Seafood Menus

FOR THE

MICROWAVE

Full-Course Meals in a Flash

Julie V. Watson

NIMBUS PUBLISHING LIMITED

Nimbus Publishing Limited
P.O. Box 9301, Station A
Halifax, Nova Scotia
B3K 5N5

Cover design: Jay Rutherford, Halifax, N.S.
Illustrations: Elizabeth Owen, Halifax, N.S.
Cover photograph: John Watson, Charlottetown, P.E.I.

Canadian Cataloging in Publication Data

Watson, Julie V., 1943-

Seafood menus for the microwave

ISBN 0-921054-44-0

1. Cookery (Seafood) 2. Microwave cookery
I. Title

TX747.W38 1990 641.6'92 C90-097535-0

Printed and bound in Canada

For Peggy, who bailed me out in a time of need,
and for Reita, who made it possible

Contents

CREDITS

Prince Edward Island Department of Fisheries
Prince Edward Island Department of Agriculture
Prince Edward Island Potato Marketing Board
British Columbia Packers Limited
Fisheries Council of British Columbia
Pillsbury Canada Limited
Safeway Stores Inc.
Canadian Egg Marketing Agency
Florida Department of Agriculture and Consumer Services
Oregon-Washington-California Pear Bureau
Canadian Living
Chatelaine
Family Circle
B.C. Woman to Woman
Good Food
Woman's Day
Better Homes & Gardens
Kasey Wilson, my mentor
Jack, my husband, who samples, creates, and tests with a smile—usually

Introduction

When we purchased our microwave, my husband and I signed up for a cooking course given by the store that sold it to us. That was the smartest move we made, because it opened our eyes to just how versatile this appliance is. Since then, I've gone to other courses and have even given a few.

The most important thing you can do with your microwave is experiment. Something may not work the first time, but if you work at it, adjusting times, frequency of stirring, covering methods, and ingredients, you can end up with one of the best recipes in your repertoire. If you use your microwave only to thaw and reheat food or to cook popcorn, you do yourself and it a disservice.

After a few years of trial and error, the microwave oven is, at long last, coming into its own. It is finally being recognized for what it is: a useful appliance that does certain things extremely well. Through experience in the home, as well as through research and testing by experts, owners are finding out more about microwave ovens.

Heading the list of foods that "work" in the microwave are seafood, particularly fish, and vegetables. Both benefit from steaming and poaching, which are so simple in the microwave, and both adapt well to fast cooking. When you cook a head of cauliflower in 5 minutes, whip up superb fish steaks in 10, and have dinner on the table in 15, you will truly begin to enjoy this appliance.

Other dishes, of course, are suited to microwave cooking: meatloaf, baked potatoes, sauces, grains, desserts, and snacks. There are, however, functions that the microwave doesn't do as well as the conventional stove and oven: baking, roasting, and sautéing.

This book offers a variety of seafood, vegetable, and dessert recipes that are simple to prepare, that use reasonably priced and easy-to-find ingredients, and that are delicious. It is in menu format to show you how to cook a whole meal in your microwave. But don't hesitate to use any recipe with something else.

The majority of the recipes keep nutrition at the forefront. For me, one of the joys of the microwave is the way it helps eliminate the "baddies" from the table. You don't need fat and sugar to obtain wonderful flavor.

Cooking in a Flash

Microwaves are a form of high-frequency radio waves produced by a tube and transmitted to the oven, where they are reflected and absorbed by the food. Like sunlight streaming through a window, they pass through some materials, such as paper, glass, and plastic. Materials such as these, which do not absorb microwaves, are ideal for using in microwave ovens.

During cooking, food absorbs microwaves, causing its molecules to vibrate at a rate of 2.45 billion times per second. The vibration causes friction, and heat is produced and conducted to the center of the food.

Clearly, the microwave oven offers a new method of cooking, but it is a practical and enjoyable one. Your microwave will work for you if you take the time to learn about it.

GENERAL RULES

KNOW YOUR OVEN No two microwave ovens are the same, so study your manual. A simple oven is all you need. A full-power, 650- to 700-watt, oven is best. In fact, most cookbooks contain recipes tested in a 700-watt oven. If yours is less than that, you may have to increase cooking time slightly.

BE PREPARED Prepare all ingredients before you begin cooking. Food cooked in the microwave tends to cool quicker than that cooked in a conventional oven because the containers don't get as hot. Therefore, before cooking, always set the table and make sure that everyone is ready to eat.

KEEP IT MOIST The peculiarities of microwave cooking cause many foods to dry out before they brown. Therefore the microwave is best for moist cooking, or steaming, poaching, and braising. This usually means covering the food as it cooks.

KEEP IT MOVING The random way microwaves strike food means that hot and cold spots can be a problem even in the newest ovens. Microwaves do not, as we are usually told, cook from the inside out but from different directions. The waves penetrate to a depth of less than 2 inches (5 cm), so the center of food is cooked by heat from the food around it. Therefore there is a possibility of unevenly cooked dishes. The simple remedy is to stir, turn, or rotate food during cooking.

You have to think in seconds and minutes, rather than quarter-hours and half-hours. Keep watch and attend to the food as if it were cooking on the stovetop.

KEEP IT HOT Every microwave should come with a warming tray. When cooking for a crowd, these tabletop appliances are wonderful tools for keeping every dish at its best.

FACTORS THAT AFFECT COOKING TIME

MOISTURE Foods that contain high degrees of moisture, such as spinach, cook faster. The opposite is also true: foods that contain less moisture, such as carrots, cook slower. The more liquid added to food, however, the longer the cooking period.

SUGAR AND FAT The amount of sugar in foods determines the degree of heat produced: the more sugar the more intense the heat and the shorter the cooking time. Higher fat content will also hasten cooking.

DENSITY Porous foods such as tomatoes, spinach, and mushrooms cook faster. Dense foods such as peas or lentils require longer periods.

TEMPERATURE Ideally, food should be at room temperature when you start cooking, as the colder it is, the longer it will take in the microwave.

PREPARATION Smaller pieces of food cook faster, but try to have all the same size.

ARRANGEMENT The arrangement of food plays an important role. Four or five potatoes arranged in a circle, for example, cook faster than if they were placed randomly. Arrangement in a circle allows even bombardment by microwaves.

UTENSILS

Pay attention to the kind of cooking containers you use. In short, you cannot use metal cookware. Most other materials, however, are acceptable: glass, china (make sure there is no gold or silver on it), pottery, paper towels (not those made of dyed or recycled paper, which may contain metal chips), plastic wrap (the package usually specifies whether it is microwave safe), and wax paper. Some plastic containers are okay, but some may melt, so use only those sold as microwave safe. To test a container, place it in the microwave oven next to, but not touching, a glass measure containing 1/2 cup (125 mL) water. Microwave at High 1 minute. If the container becomes hot, it should not be used.

COVERING

Foods that benefit from steam, such as fruits, vegetables, and fish, should be tightly covered with a fitted lid, or plastic wrap folded back to create a vent, or opening, about an inch (2.5 cm) long. If you want excess moisture to escape, cover food loosely with wax paper to protect the microwave from splatters. A paper towel is sometimes useful to absorb moisture. Bacon- or crumb-coated fish fillets, for example, should be covered with a paper towel.

ROTATING

Some ovens are equipped with automatic rotating trays. Others are not, and therefore some dishes may require manual rotation during cooking.

STANDING TIME

Many recipes tell you to let food stand after cooking; food should be left covered but may be removed from the oven. Because the microwave process of cooking is through intense molecular vibration, food continues to cook even after the oven has been turned off. The length of that process depends on the ingredients, the amount of bulk, and so on. It's important to remember this extended cooking time—the time that allows the molecules to stop vibrating—especially with delicate foods such as fish.

SEQUENCING

Timing is the key to successfully preparing a meal in the microwave. It may appear complex at first but, with a bit of practice, becomes as simple as reading recipes.

Start with dishes that need to be cooled after cooking. (Many desserts fall into this category.) Continue with dishes that require standing time. During standing time, microwave quick-cooking foods, such as vegetables or fish.

Remember, not all dishes have to be done in the microwave. Salads, obviously, and certain other recipes are best prepared conventionally, and they round out a meal, especially one for a large crowd. Some dishes also benefit from the use of both the microwave and the conventional oven.

CONVERTING RECIPES

Some recipes for the conventional oven can be done in the microwave, but it requires experimenting. Generally, dishes that cook covered, by steaming, poaching, or in a sauce, work well. (To figure out times, check similar recipes in your microwave manual-cookbook.) Use less seasoning, especially salt (it's better to season afterwards than to ruin a dish), and use less liquid, especially in casseroles. Liquids do not reduce so much during microwave cooking.

SEAFOOD HINTS AND PROBLEM SOLVERS

DEFROSTING Defrost packages of fish. Place frozen package on a double layer of paper towel and place in center of tray in microwave oven. Set oven on Defrost or Medium (50%). Turn package once during cooking time. One pound (500 g) fish usually takes 3 minutes to defrost enough to separate fillets under cold water. Microwave immediately.

WASHING Before microwaving a whole fish or a thick piece of fish, wash it in cold salted water. Use 1/4 cup (50 mL) coarse salt to 6 to 8 cups (1.5 to 2 L) cold water. Let fish stand a few minutes and remove from water. Wipe off excess water with paper towel.

ARRANGEMENT Place fish steaks or fillets in a spoke design on a glass pie plate. Make sure thicker portions are toward outer edges. Fold over thin ends to achieve uniform thickness. Cover with plastic wrap, leaving a vent.

COOKING TIME For each lb (500 g) fish, including stuffing if used, microwave at High 4 to 5 minutes. Rotate dish at halfway point. To prevent overcooking, remove fish from microwave when outer areas flake and become opaque. Inner areas will finish cooking during standing time. The secret to successfully cooking fish is not to overcook. Cooking in the microwave means low evaporation, guaranteeing moist, flavorful fish every time.

STANDING TIME If you cook fish until it is "done," then it will overcook during standing time. Generally, 1 lb (500 g) fish should stand, covered, 2 to 5 minutes after cooking. Take salmon loaf, for example. It stands 5 minutes, and that is long enough to cook vegetables or a white sauce.

PERFECT POACHING Prepare a tasty meal by poaching fish and serving it with a simple sauce made by combining equal amounts of sour cream and yogurt with a favorite herb. Place room-temperature fish steaks or fillets or a small whole fish in a glass pie plate. Almost cover with poaching liquid (water, water-wine combination, or tomato juice, etc.). Cover with plastic wrap, leaving a vent. Microwave at High 6 to 8 minutes per lb (500 g).

FISH SAUCE Put poaching liquid in a glass measure (no more than half full) and microwave at High until liquid is reduced by half. Stir in a little butter, seasoning, and parsley. The concentrated flavor is delightful.

SOUPS FOR SAUCES Two or three sauces in this book call for canned soups as a base. Usually it isn't worth the effort, time, or expense to try to duplicate what comes in the can. Most soups are high in salt, so be cautious about adding any more. Try to use low-sodium, low-calorie soups.

REHEATING To reheat fish, arrange on a plate with the thicker portions toward the rim of the plate. Add sauce or butter where desired. Cover with wax paper and microwave at Medium-High (70%) 2 to 3 minutes, checking after 2.

STEAMING CLAMS, MUSSELS, SMALL BAY SCALLOPS Refer to Cavendish seafood bake (see index) or use the following method. Rinse and drain shellfish. Place as many as will fit around edge of a glass pie plate. Cover with plastic wrap, vent, and microwave at High 2 to 4 minutes or until shellfish open. If some do not open, try cooking another minute. Then discard those that don't open. Reserve liquid for a shellfish dip.

If shellfish are tough, next time try reducing power to 50%.

SHELLFISH DIP Use method for fish sauce (above) to create a dipping sauce for mussels or clams. Strain liquid before reducing.

INSTANT MAIN MEAL Leftovers, canned salmon or tuna, or quick-cooking shrimp can be added to a commercial or prepared sauce. For example, add shrimp and/or leftover mussels to spaghetti sauce and serve with spaghetti squash.

Meals for Two

FALL MEDLEY

Fall always brings some cool wet days that make us glad to be back in the kitchen after a summer of outdoor living. On P.E.I., it seems to happen about the same time that pears and potatoes are harvested; the trout are plump and succulent.

MENU
Lime-and-Dill Trout Fillets
Mushroom-Stuffed Potatoes
Golden Pear Pie

SEQUENCE
1. Preheat conventional oven to 425°F (220°C) while preparing and microwaving golden pear pie.

2. When pie is done in microwave, place in conventional oven. While pie is baking, microwave potatoes. Both are done about same time.

3. While potatoes are cooking, prepare lime-and-dill trout fillets, as well as mushroom stuffing.

4. Remove pie from conventional oven and set aside to cool.

5. When potatoes are done, microwave trout fillets. Meanwhile, stuff potatoes.

6. Remove trout fillets from oven and microwave stuffed potatoes 1 minute per potato.

Lime-and-Dill Trout Fillets

Enjoy the peach-pink, tender flesh of a trout fillet.

    1 *large or 2 small trout fillets (about 1 lb/500 g)* 1
    1 *lime* 1
    Fresh dill weed, snipped
    Green onion, finely chopped
    Freshly ground pepper
    1 *green pepper, cut into rings* 1
    2 *medium-size tomatoes, halved* 2
    Butter

Place trout fillets in a large pie plate, cutting large fillets in half if necessary. Squeeze lime juice over fillets. Sprinkle with dill weed and green onion. Sprinkle pepper over all. At ends or in open spots, place 4 green-pepper rings. Place half a tomato in each. Dab butter on each tomato and sprinkle with pepper. Lay a few thin slices of lime on fillets if desired.

Cover with plastic wrap, leaving a vent to one side. Microwave at High 4 to 6 minutes, depending on thickness of fillets. Let stand 2 minutes, then test with a fork to make sure fillets flake easily at thickest point.

To serve, carefully lift any surface bones off fillets and discard. Lift away fillets from skin and place on hot dinner plates. Carefully add pepper rings with tomatoes.

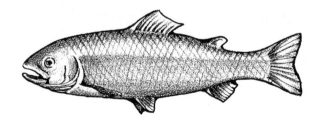

Mushroom-Stuffed Potatoes

Try out this dish on your family, then serve it to company.

> 4 *baking potatoes of uniform size* 4
> **Mushroom Stuffing:**
> 1/4 cup *butter* 50 mL
> 1/2 cup *finely chopped onion* 125 mL
> 1/4 cup *finely chopped celery* 50 mL
> 2 tbsp *finely chopped green or red peppers* 25 mL
> 2 cups *chopped fresh mushrooms* 500 mL
> 1/4 cup *finely chopped fresh parsley*
>   *or 1 tbsp (15 mL) dried* 50 mL
> 1 tbsp *milk, sour cream, or yogurt* 15 mL
> *Pepper*
> 1/2 cup *grated Cheddar cheese* 125 mL

Wash potatoes, dry, and prick with a fork. Arrange in a circle on a double layer of paper towel. Cover with wax paper. Microwave at High 12 to 16 minutes. Let stand, covered, until tender.

Prepare stuffing. In a bowl, microwave butter, uncovered, at High 1 minute. Add onion, celery, peppers, and mushrooms. Microwave at High 2 to 3 minutes, stirring once.

Cut slice from top of each potato. Scoop out pulp, preserving shells, and mash with sautéed stuffing. Blend in parsley, milk, and pepper. Spoon mixture into potato shells, smoothing tops. (Freeze at this point if desired.) Sprinkle with cheese and microwave, uncovered, at High 1 minute per potato or until cheese melts.

Note: If potatoes are prepared ahead of time and refrigerated, increase final cooking time by 30 seconds per potato. If frozen, microwave one potato at High 3 to 4 minutes; 2 potatoes, 5 to 6 minutes; 3 potatoes, 7 to 8 minutes; 4 potatoes, 8 to 9 minutes.

Golden Pear Pie

> 4 *fresh pears, peeled if desired, cored, and sliced* 4
> *Lemon juice*
> 1/2 cup *dried apricots* 125 mL
> 1/2 cup *packed brown sugar* 125 mL
> 2 tbsp *flour* 25 mL
> 1/4 cup *chopped pecans* 50 mL
> 1/4 tsp *ground cinnamon* 1 mL
> Dash *salt* Dash
> *Pastry for 2-crust 9-inch (22.5-cm) pie*
> 2 tbsp *butter or margarine* 25 mL

In a bowl, sprinkle pears with lemon juice and set aside. In a pot, cover apricots with water. Bring to a boil on stovetop and simmer 10 minutes. Drain and dice.

In a separate bowl, combine pears, apricots, brown sugar, flour, pecans, cinnamon, and salt. Turn into pastry-lined pie plate; dot with butter. Adjust top crust, seal and flute edges, and cut vents into top crust. Microwave at High 10 to 12 minutes or until filling is bubbly. Bake in conventional oven at 425°F (220°C) 10 to 15 minutes or until golden brown.

Note: This recipe was developed for a 600- to 700-watt microwave oven. To cook conventionally, bake at 425°F (220°C) 45 to 50 minutes or until golden brown.

PROVENCE FARE

The meaty texture of swordfish, not to mention its pristine white color, is complemented by ratatouille, the vegetable stew that originated in Provençe. Parmesan garlic bread is the pièce de résistance.

MENU
Grilled Swordfish Steaks
Ratatouille
Parmesan Garlic Bread
Strawberry-Apricot Compote

SEQUENCE
1.   Prepare strawberry-apricot compote and chill.

2.   Prepare Parmesan garlic bread.

3.   Prepare ratatouille and microwave to stage of adding tomatoes. While ratatouille is cooking, prepare swordfish steaks.

4.   Remove ratatouille from oven and microwave swordfish steaks, following directions for browning dish. Meanwhile, broil garlic bread or toast in toaster oven.

5.   When swordfish steaks are done, remove from microwave and set aside. Add tomatoes to ratatouille and finish cooking.

6.   Place swordfish steaks and garlic bread on hot serving plates and set on table. Remove ratatouille from microwave and enjoy.

Grilled Swordfish Steaks

We were given this recipe at the cooking classes that came with our microwave. I was intrigued by the use of the browning dish, which is normally used for hamburgers or grilled sandwiches. In summer, we love to barbecue swordfish. This was a winter bonus.

> 2 *swordfish steaks (about 1 lb/500 g)* 2
> 1 tbsp *vegetable oil* 15 mL
> *Lemon pepper*
> *Paprika*

Preheat a 9-inch (22.5-cm) browning dish in microwave at High 5 minutes. Brush 1 side of swordfish steaks with oil. Sprinkle with lemon pepper and paprika. Place seasoned side down on pre-heated browning dish. Cover loosely with plastic wrap, leaving a vent. Microwave at High 1 to 2 minutes or until swordfish flakes. Turn over, cover, and let stand 2 minutes. To serve, turn seasoned side up.

Ratatouille

The flavors of the vegetables meld in the microwave, yet each retains its shape. Ratatouille is not usually teamed with fish, but they make a delightful combination. This recipe makes enough for four people. Save the leftovers and eat it cold the next day. It's great.

3 tbsp *olive oil* 50 mL
1 *large red onion, thinly sliced* 1
4 *cloves garlic, minced* 4
1 *medium-size eggplant, peeled and cut into*
    l-inch (2.5-cm) cubes 1
3 *small zucchinis, trimmed and cut into 1/2-inch (1-cm) slices* 3
1 *medium-size sweet green pepper, seeded and cut into strips* 1
1/4 cup *fresh basil or 4 tsp (20 mL) dried* 50 mL
Freshly ground black pepper to taste
2 *large ripe tomatoes, cored and cut into wedges* 2
Salt (optional)

In a 2-qt (2-L) casserole, combine oil, onion, and garlic. Micro-wave, uncovered, at High 2 minutes. Add eggplant, zucchini, green pepper, basil, and black pepper. Stir gently, then cover tightly with lid. Microwave at High 3 minutes. Stir in tomatoes, re-cover, and microwave at High 1 more minute. Taste and add salt or pepper if desired. Serves 4.

Parmesan Garlic Bread

Garlic butter
Italian bread or Italian rolls, halved
Grated Parmesan cheese

Spread garlic butter on bread. Sprinkle with Parmesan, and toast in toaster oven or broil in conventional oven.

Strawberry-Apricot Compote

This light dessert clears the palate.

1/4 cup *dry white wine* 50 mL
1/4 cup *cranberry juice* 50 mL
Strips lemon zest
1 tsp *minced crystallized ginger* 5 mL
6 *dried apricots, cut into thin strips* 6
1/8 tsp *vanilla extract* 1 mL
4 *fresh strawberries, hulled and quartered* 4

In a small bowl, combine wine, cranberry juice, one 2-inch by 1/2-inch (5-cm by 1-cm) strip lemon zest, and ginger. Microwave, uncovered, at High 2 minutes. Add apricots and microwave at High 1 minute. Stir in vanilla. Let cool to room temperature, then refrigerate at least 1 hour or until cold. Remove lemon zest and stir in strawberries. Divide into 2 champagne glasses. Garnish with fresh strips lemon zest. Serve cold.

FULL-DAY PAMPER

The profusion of vegetables teams perfectly with salmon steaks smothered with a delicious and unusual sauce. You can prepare the vegetables and the dessert the night before, so this meal is perfect for those busy days when you deserve a treat but are too busy to labor for hours.

MENU
Salmon Steaks with Havarti-and-Artichoke Sauce
Oriental Vegetables
Buster Sundae Pie

SEQUENCE
1. The night before or several hours ahead of time, prepare buster sundae pie.

2. Prepare vegetables for Oriental vegetables and store in plastic bag (mushrooms are best when not sliced more than 2 or 3 hours before).

3. At mealtime, prepare ingredients for salmon steaks with Havarti-and-artichoke sauce, as well as remaining ingredients for vegetables.

4. Microwave vegetables. Remove from oven and microwave salmon steaks. Meanwhile, top vegetables with sesame seeds and cover.

5. When salmon steaks are cooked, remove from oven and cover. Prepare and microwave Havarti-and-artichoke sauce. While sauce is in for final cooking, check salmon steaks to see if done by inserting fork at bone; meat should come away easily. If necessary, microwave salmon steaks and vegetables 1 more minute.

Salmon Steaks with Havarti-and-Artichoke Sauce

2 *salmon steaks (about 8 oz/250 g each)* 2
Havarti and Artichoke Sauce:
1 tbsp *butter* 15 mL
1 tbsp *flour* 15 mL
3/4 cup *milk* 175 mL
1/4 cup *coarsely chopped artichoke hearts,*
   canned or fresh 50 mL
1/4 cup *grated Havarti cheese* 50 mL
2 *drops Tabasco Sauce* 2

In a baking dish, arrange salmon steaks with "legs" to center. Cover loosely with paper towel and microwave at High 4 to 5 minutes. Cover and set aside.

Prepare sauce. Place butter and flour in a small bowl; microwave, uncovered, at High 1 minute. Slowly stir in milk and microwave at High 3 to 4 minutes or until mixture has bubbled and thickened, stirring once or twice. Stir in artichoke hearts, Havarti, and Tabasco. Microwave at High 30 seconds. Serve hot alongside or over salmon.

Oriental Vegetables

1 tsp *butter or margarine* 5 mL
2/3 cup *bite-size broccoli pieces* 150 mL
2/3 cup *sliced mushrooms* 150 mL
2 tbsp *chopped onion* 25 mL
1 tsp *soy sauce* 5 mL
1 tsp *sesame seeds (optional)* 5 mL

In a 1-qt (1-L) casserole, microwave butter, uncovered, at High 30 to 40 seconds or until bubbly. Add remaining ingredients, except sesame seeds, and microwave, covered, at High 2-1/2 to 3 minutes, stirring halfway through. Sprinkle with sesame seeds if desired and let stand, covered, 1 minute.

Buster Sundae Pie

The Pillsbury pie crust for this recipe has to be only unfolded and cooked in the microwave. As this pie serves eight, there's lots left over, but do not freeze for more than a few days.

> 1 *Pillsbury All Ready pie crust* 1
> 1 qt *vanilla ice cream, softened slightly* 1 L
> 1/2 cup *caramel topping* 125 mL
> 1/2 cup *fudge or chocolate topping* 125 mL
> 3/4 cup *unsalted Spanish peanuts* 175 mL
> *Whipped cream (optional)*
> *Long-stemmed maraschino cherries (optional)*

Microwave crust according to directions and let cool. Spread half of ice cream over crust. Drizzle with half of each topping. Sprinkle with peanuts. Cover with remaining ice cream, then drizzle with remaining topping. Freeze several hours or overnight. Cut into wedges and garnish with whipped cream and cherries if desired. Serves 8.

SOUP 'N' SWEET

Lunch or even a late dinner requires little more than a super soup and a delicious dessert to nourish and satisfy. This shrimp, tomato, green-chili, and lime creation needs nothing else to make a meal. The pecan-stuffed apples are sheer luxury.

MENU
Shrimp, Tomato, Green-Chili, and Lime Soup
Pecan-Stuffed Apples

SEQUENCE
1.   Stuff apples.

2.   Prepare and microwave soup.

3.   While soup is standing, microwave stuffed apples and leave in oven until ready to serve.

Shrimp, Tomato, Green-Chili, and Lime Soup

When served with fresh bread and butter, this is perfect for lunch.

> 1 *small onion, finely chopped* 1
> 1 *small clove garlic, crushed* 1
> 1 tbsp *olive oil* 15 mL
> 1/2 tsp *ground cumin* 2 mL
> 1/2 tsp *chili powder* 2 mL
> 1/2 cup *chicken broth* 125 mL
> 1 *14-1/2-oz can whole tomatoes, coarsely chopped,*
>   *with liquid* 400 mL
> 1 tbsp *chopped canned mild or hot chilies* 15 mL
> 8 *large shrimp, shelled and deveined* 8
> 1 *lime* 1
> 1 tbsp *coarsely chopped coriander leaves* 15 mL
> 2 tbsp *sour cream* 25 mL

In a bowl, combine onion, garlic, and olive oil. Microwave, uncovered, at High 3 minutes, stirring once halfway through. Add cumin and chili powder and stir until completely blended. Add chicken broth, tomatoes with liquid, chilies, and shrimp. Microwave at High, uncovered, about 4 minutes or until shrimp are pink and soup is very hot.

Cut 2 thin slices from center of lime and reserve for garnish.

Squeeze juice from remaining lime halves into soup and stir in coriander. Divide into 2 bowls. Garnish soup with a dollop of sour cream and a lime slice.

Pecan-Stuffed Apples

> 2 *McIntosh or cooking apples* 2
> 1/4 cup *unsweetened apple juice* 50 mL
> 1 tbsp *unsalted butter* 15 mL
> 1 tsp *honey* 5 mL
> 1 tsp *fresh lemon juice* 5 mL
> Pinch *ground cinnamon* Pinch
> 2 *cinnamon sticks* 2
> 1/4 cup *chopped pecans* 50 mL
> *Ice cream*

Core apples from stem end, leaving bottom intact, and place on a pie plate. Place apple juice, butter, honey, lemon juice, and ground cinnamon in a 1-cup (250-mL) measure or bowl. Microwave, uncovered, at High 1 minute or until butter is melted. Pour 1 spoonful of sauce into each apple. Place 1 cinnamon stick and half of nuts into each and top with remaining sauce. Microwave, uncovered, at High 2 minutes. Tilt plate and spoon liquid over apples. Microwave at High 2 more minutes. Serve with ice cream.

TWO FOR TROUT

This satisfying meal is perfect for two on a cold, blustery fall day. Cooked this way, trout fillets retain their delicate flavor, which is too easily lost during pan frying. Go easy on the ginger and lemon: you want only to enhance the trout. When we have fresh ginger in the house, we like to grate it over the fillets instead of using powdered ginger.

MENU
Jack's Trout Fillet for Two
Cheesy Chive Potatoes
Beefsteak Tomatoes au Gratin
Chocolate-Dipped Grapefruit

SEQUENCE
1.   Prepare chocolate-dipped grapefruit and refrigerate.

2.   Prepare beefsteak tomatoes au gratin and microwave to stage where cheese is added. While tomatoes are cooking, prepare trout fillets and potatoes.

3.   Remove tomatoes from oven and microwave trout fillets. While trout fillets are cooking, put topping on tomatoes.

4.   Remove trout when done and microwave potatoes. If you have a two-tier shelf, put tomatoes back in at same time to melt cheese. If not, microwave potatoes, then finish cooking tomatoes.

Note: If you reduce quantities in potato and tomato recipes, be sure to decrease cooking time.

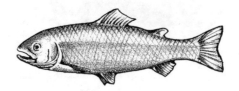

Jack's Trout Fillet for Two

Fish farming is not only providing a year-round supply of wonderful fresh trout, it is also producing such plump, large fish that one fillet is large enough to feed two.

> 1 *large or 2 small trout fillets* 1
> *Ground ginger*
> *Lemon pepper*
> 1 *lime* 1

Lay trout skin side down on a large pie plate or in a shallow baking dish. Remove any visible large bones but don't tear flesh. Dust lightly with ginger and lemon pepper. Squeeze juice from half of lime over fish. Cover with plastic wrap, leaving a vent. Microwave at High 6 minutes, turning a quarter turn twice. Let stand 2 minutes before serving.

Cheesy Chive Potatoes

Use leftover boiled or baked potatoes or the pulp from making potato skins.

> 3 cups *mashed potatoes* 750 mL
> 1/2 cup *cottage cheese* 125 mL
> 1 tbsp *chopped chives* 15 mL
> *Salt and pepper*

In a bowl, combine all ingredients. Cover with plastic wrap and microwave at High 4 to 5 minutes, turning bowl once. Serves 2 to 4.

Beefsteak Tomatoes au Gratin

When choosing tomatoes to microwave, select medium-size ones (about 6 oz/175 g each). They must also be firm and ripe, as juicier tomatoes will disintegrate during cooking. The best are those purchased at a farmer's market or grown in your garden. Those packaged in plastic and shipped across the country are picked green and lack the flavor necessary to serve as a hot side dish.

>   4 *beefsteak tomatoes* 4
>   8 *1/8-inch (3-mm) thick slices sharp Cheddar,*
>   *Swiss, or Gruyère cheese* 8

Halve tomatoes crosswise but do not peel. Arrange in a circle on a platter, cut sides up and not touching. Cover with plastic wrap and leave a vent at one end. Microwave at High 5 to 6 minutes or until tomatoes are slightly softened, rotating platter a half turn at half time. Cut cheese slices slightly smaller than tomato halves. Top each tomato half with 1 cheese slice and microwave, uncovered, at Medium High (70%) 1-1/2 to 2 minutes or until cheese melts. Serves 4.

Chocolate-Dipped Grapefruit

This low-calorie dessert is simple to make, and the combination of flavors is wonderful.

>   8 *grapefruit sections* 8
>   1 oz *semisweet chocolate* 30 g

Pat grapefruit sections dry with paper towels. Place chocolate in a small bowl and microwave, uncovered, at Medium (50%) 2 minutes. Stir. Microwave at Medium (50%) another 30 seconds or until smooth and melted. Dip each grapefruit section in chocolate, turning to coat 1/3 of section. If desired, use a knife to spread evenly. Lay on a plate or cookie sheet covered with wax paper and refrigerate 30 minutes before serving.

NOVA SCOTIAN COD DINNER

Years ago, on a small island off the coast of Nova Scotia, we enjoyed a simple meal that our hosts loved to find on the table at the end of a hard day. Salted cod was usually served because it stored easily. For the following adaptation, I suggest you poach fresh cod fillets. Traditionally, an egg sauce was served over peas and the fish; mashed potatoes and homemade bread rounded out the meal.

MENU
Cod Fillets and Peas
Egg Sauce
Pear-Cheese Crisp

SEQUENCE
1.	Prepare and microwave pear-cheese crisp. While crisp is cooking, preheat conventional oven for browning.

2.	Assemble ingredients for egg sauce and prepare cod fillets and peas.

3.	Peel hard-boiled eggs.

4.	Remove crisp from microwave and brown in conventional oven, putting in 2 serving dishes to warm.

5.	Prepare and microwave egg sauce, then microwave fish and peas.

Note: If in a hurry to eat, microwave crisp while eating first course. Brown while table is being cleared and kettle is boiling for tea.

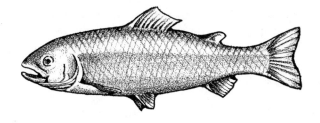

Cod Fillets and Peas

Serve this dish with mashed potatoes, either on a hot platter or on individual hot plates.

>   2 *cod fillets* 2
>   *Butter*
>   *Salt to taste*
>   *Freshly ground pepper to taste*
>   *Peas*

Place fillets in a pie plate. Dot with butter and sprinkle with salt and pepper.

Place peas in a small bowl, adding a little water if using frozen or fresh peas. Place bowl in center of pie plate, arranging fillets around bowl. (If your oven has a 2-tier shelf, place peas on top shelf, covering peas and fish with plastic wrap.) Cover with plastic wrap, leaving a vent. Microwave at High 3-1/2 to 6 minutes, depending on thickness of fillets.

Egg Sauce

>   2 tbsp *butter or margarine* 25 mL
>   3 tbsp *flour* 50 mL
>   1/4 tsp *salt* 1 mL
>   1/8 tsp *white pepper* 1 mL
>   1 cup *milk* 250 mL
>   1 tsp *prepared or Dijon mustard with seeds, or to taste* 5 mL
>   2 *hard-boiled eggs, chopped* 2
>   *Seasoning to taste*

In a 1-qt (1-L) measure, microwave butter, uncovered, at High 45 to 60 seconds. Stir in flour, salt, and pepper. Microwave at High 2 to 2-1/2 minutes, stirring several times. (If thicker sauce is desired, continue cooking at High in 20-second sequences, stirring after each.) Stir in mustard, eggs, and seasoning. Pour over cod fillets and peas. Makes about 1 cup (250 mL).

Note: Make other sauces by leaving out eggs and adding cheese, cooked mushrooms, cooked onions, spices, tomato paste, herbs, or horseradish to a basic white sauce.

Pear-Cheese Crisp

This recipe adds a new dimension to an old-fashioned crisp.

4 cups *cored and sliced fresh pears, peeled if desired* 1 L
1 tsp *vanilla* 5 mL
1/2 cup *shredded sharp Cheddar cheese* 125 mL
1/2 cup *flour* 125 mL
1/2 cup *quick-cooking rolled oats* 125 mL
1/2 cup *packed brown sugar* 125 mL
1/4 cup *butter or margarine, softened* 50 mL

Toss pears with vanilla and place in buttered baking dish that is about 2 inches (5 cm) deep. Sprinkle with cheese. In a bowl, combine flour, rolled oats, and brown sugar. Cut in butter until mixture resembles coarse crumbs. Sprinkle over pears. Microwave, uncovered, at High 10 to 12 minutes or until pears are tender. Bake in a conventional oven at 425°F (220°C) 8 to 10 minutes or until crust is golden brown. Serves 6.

Meals for Four

PASTA WITH SMOKED SALMON

This super dinner dispels any feeling of simplicity by the luxurious addition of smoked salmon.

MENU
Fettuccine with Smoked-Salmon Sauce
Brussels Sprouts
Lemon Bars

SEQUENCE
1. Prepare and microwave lemon bars the evening or morning before.

2. Prepare brussel sprouts.

3. Assemble ingredients for fettuccine and smoked-salmon sauce. Cook pasta. Meanwhile, microwave cream cheese for sauce.

4. When cream cheese is done, microwave brussel sprouts. Meanwhile, complete sauce.

Fettuccine with Smoked-Salmon Sauce

This is an instant dish. We buy fresh pasta at the farmer's market:
it requires only 2 to 3 minutes' cooking.

1 pkg *fettuccine or spaghetti* 1 pkg
Smoked-Salmon Sauce:
6 oz *cream cheese* 175 g
1 cup *milk* 250 mL
6 oz *sliced smoked salmon, cut into small squares* 175 g
2 tsp *lemon juice* 10 mL
1/2 tsp *dried dill weed* 2 mL

In a pot, cook fettuccine according to directions. Meanwhile,
prepare smoked-salmon sauce. Place cream cheese in a deep
1-1/2-qt (1.5-L) bowl and microwave, uncovered, at Medium
(50%) 45 seconds or until soft. Using a whisk, beat until creamy.
Gradually whisk in milk. Stir in smoked salmon, lemon juice, and
dill weed. Spoon over fettuccine.

Note: Some pasta, especially fresh, sticks together after draining.
If necessary, drizzle with a small amount of olive oil.

Brussel Sprouts

1 lb *brussel sprouts, washed and blemished leaves*
    removed 500 g
1/4 cup *water* 50 mL

Arrange brussel sprouts in a round dish, with larger ones on
outside and smaller in middle. Add water, cover, and microwave
at High 6 to 8 minutes, checking if done after 6. Drain and serve.

Lemon Bars

Tart and delicate, these are great either with ice cream or alone. Serve at room temperature, and for best results, use imperial measures.

> *Non-stick vegetable-oil cooking spray*
> **Crust:**
> 1/2 cup *butter or margarine at room temperature* 125 mL
> 1/4 cup *icing sugar* 50 mL
> 1 cup *flour* 250 mL
> 1/8 tsp *salt* 1 mL
> **Topping:**
> 2 *large eggs* 2
> 1 cup *granulated sugar* 250 mL
> 1 tsp *freshly grated lemon peel* 5 mL
> 1/4 cup *freshly squeezed lemon juice* 50 mL
> 2 tbsp *flour* 25 mL
> 1/8 tsp *baking powder* 1 mL

Spray bottom of an 8-inch (20-cm) square baking dish with vegetable oil. Prepare crust. In a medium-size bowl, beat together butter and sugar. Stir in flour and salt until blended. With lightly floured fingertips, press mixture evenly in bottom of baking dish. Place dish on an inverted saucer (or microwave-safe trivet) and microwave, uncovered, at High 3 to 5 minutes, rotating dish a half-turn halfway through cooking. (Crust will appear dry on top with some wet spots on bottom. It will not be browned.) Let stand about 15 minutes or until slightly cooled.

Prepare topping. In a small bowl, lightly beat eggs. Stir in remaining ingredients until well blended. Pour over crust. Microwave, uncovered, at High 3 to 5 minutes, turning a half-turn once. (Edges should be set. Top will have some foamy spots, and center will be slightly loose. It will set on standing.) Cool completely before cutting into bars. Remove carefully.

PRINCE EDWARD ISLAND SPUDS 'N' SCALLOPS

Our country home in Prince Edward Island is often bordered by crops of potatoes, so they are a regular part of our diet. Not far away, fishermen bring in some of the most succulent scallops found anywhere. They are large compared with many on the market.

MENU
Scallops with Sesame-Seed Topping
Asparagus with Ginger Butter
Baked Potatoes with Garnish
Strawberry-Orange Chocolate Drizzle

SEQUENCE
1. Prepare fruit for strawberry-orange chocolate drizzle and assemble ingredients for chocolate sauce.

2. Microwave potatoes. Meanwhile, prepare asparagus.

3. When potatoes are done, set aside. Microwave asparagus and prepare scallops.

4. When asparagus is done, microwave scallops. Meanwhile, make ginger butter and complete asparagus.

5. Split potatoes and garnish. Complete scallops with sesame-seed topping. If asparagus has cooled, microwave 1 more minute.

6. After main course, clear table, and while coffee is brewing, prepare and microwave chocolate sauce.

Scallops with Sesame-Seed Topping

This Prince Edward Island recipe is sweet and delicious. Microwaving, covered, at Medium (50%) allows the scallops to cook evenly, without stirring. Judge cooking time by the size of the scallops, and check at the 4-minute mark. Scallops are done when they become opaque and spring back when lightly squeezed.

> 2 tbsp *butter* 25 mL
> 1 lb *scallops* 500 g
> 2 tbsp *dry bread crumbs* 25 mL
> 1/4 tsp *pepper* 1 mL
> 1 tbsp *sesame seeds* 15 mL
> 1/4 tsp *salt (optional)* 1 mL

Place butter on a 9- to 10-inch (22.5- to 25-cm) pie plate. Microwave, uncovered, at High 30 to 45 seconds or until melted. Stir scallops into butter to coat tops and bottoms. Arrange scallops in a ring at outside of pie plate. Sprinkle with bread crumbs, pepper, sesame seeds, and salt. Cover with paper towel. Microwave at Medium (50%) 4 to 6-1/2 minutes or until opaque and resilient to touch. Let stand, covered, 2 minutes.

Asparagus with Ginger Butter

> 1 lb *asparagus tips with tough ends snapped off* 500 g
> 1 tbsp *soft butter* 15 mL
> 1 tsp *freshly squeezed lemon juice* 5 mL
> 1/4 tsp *finely grated fresh ginger root* 1 mL
> *Freshly ground black pepper to taste*

Gently wash asparagus in cold water. Without drying, place in a dish just large enough to hold them. Cover with lid or vented plastic wrap. Microwave at High 3 to 3-1/2 minutes or until tender-crisp but not soft. Meanwhile, combine remaining ingredients until well blended. Drain asparagus and spread with butter mixture, turning until all are coated.

Baked Potatoes with Garnish

Baked potatoes can be spruced up with a simple garnish. Russet Burbanks bake well and have a mealy, white flesh suitable for garnishes.

> 4 *clean baking potatoes* 4
> *Sour cream*
> *Chopped chives*

Prick potatoes with a fork. Arrange in a circle on tray and cover with paper towel. Microwave at High 12 to 16 minutes, rearranging and turning during cooking. Let stand, covered, 3 to 5 minutes or until tender. Garnish with sour cream and chives or your favorite garnish (yogurt, toasted sesame seeds, diced red or green peppers, whipped butter, chopped parsley, or salsa).

Note: If desired, to make crispier skins, place potatoes in a toaster oven at 450°F (230°C) during standing time.

Strawberry-Orange Chocolate Drizzle

Any combination of fruit will work, but the blend of orange and chocolate when served with a good coffee is especially delicious. To wow guests, heat the sauce just before serving. It's scrumptious warm.

> *Strawberries, hulled*
> *Orange wedges*
> **Chocolate Sauce:**
> 1/4 cup *heavy cream* 50 mL
> 4 oz *semisweet chocolate pieces* 125 g
> 1 tbsp *vanilla extract* 15 mL

Place fruit in serving glasses. Prepare sauce. Place cream and chocolate in a 2-cup (500-mL) measure. Microwave, uncovered, at High 3 minutes, stirring every 60 seconds or until smooth. Remove from microwave and stir in vanilla extract. Pour over fruit. Makes 1 cup (250 mL) sauce.

LEMON LOVERS' DELIGHT

I love lemon. I like its tang, and I'm not wishy-washy about it. That's why this salmon loaf is tops on my list. I squeeze more lemon juice on it before eating, and then I squeeze some on green vegetables such as green beans. If you like a more subtle taste of lemon, reduce the amount of juice and zest. The potato recipe works wonders.

MENU
Lemon-Curry Salmon Loaf
Oyster Scalloped Potatoes
Super Salad
Blueberry-Lemon Cheesecake

SEQUENCE
1. Make salad and set aside.

2. Make dessert and set aside.

3. Prepare and microwave oyster scalloped potatoes, reducing cooking time by 2 minutes. While potatoes are cooking, prepare lemon-curry salmon loaf.

4. Remove potatoes from oven and microwave salmon loaf.

5. While salmon loaf is standing, finish microwaving potatoes.

Lemon-Curry Salmon Loaf

We like the combination of lemon and curry; you can use more or less as desired. Serve with a tossed green salad and light dressing.

> 1 *15-1/2-oz can salmon* 439 g
> 1 *egg, lightly beaten* 1
> 1 cup *fresh bread crumbs* 250 mL
> 1/4 cup *whipping or sour cream* 50 mL
> 2 tbsp *minced celery leaves* 25 mL
> 1/2 tsp *curry powder* 2 mL
> 3 *green onions, sliced thin* 3
> 1/4 tsp *salt* 1 mL
> *Juice and zest 1 lemon*
> *Pepper (optional)*

Place salmon (including broth and bones) in a bowl. Crush bones and skin and flake fish. Add remaining ingredients, mixing well. Place in a loaf pan. Cover with wax paper and microwave at High 6 to 9 minutes. Let stand 5 minutes. Serves 4 to 6.

Oyster Scalloped Potatoes

> 3 *medium-size potatoes, peeled and cut into*
>   *1/8-inch (3-mm) slices (about 3 cups/750 mL)* 3
> 1 *10-oz can oyster soup, undiluted* 284 mL
> *Pepper to taste*
> 1 tbsp *grated Parmesan cheese* 15 mL
> *Parsley flakes*

In a 2-qt (2-L) casserole, combine potatoes, oyster soup, and pepper. Cover and microwave at High 11 to 12 minutes or until cooked, stirring once halfway through. Sprinkle with Parmesan and parsley. Cover and let stand 3 to 4 minutes.

Super Salad

Cabbage has the advantages of being readily available and of being low in cost, yet it is usually overlooked as a salad ingredient, except in coleslaw. A brief cooking in the microwave makes it more acceptable in salads.

> Half head (small) red cabbage, cored and shredded
> Sliced mushrooms
> Sliced sweet red pepper
> Canned chickpeas
> Salad dressing or vinaigrette

Wrap cabbage in plastic wrap and place on a paper plate. Microwave at High 2 minutes. Drain, rinse, and pat dry. Combine cabbage with other ingredients and top salad with your favorite dressing.

Blueberry-Lemon Cheesecake

Use a premade pie crust that can be microwaved or a ready-to-use graham-cracker crust as the base for this yummy dessert.

> 1 *Pillsbury All Ready pie crust* 1
> 1 *8-oz pkg Philadelphia cream cheese, softened* 250 g
> 1/3 cup *sugar* 75 mL
> 1 to 2 tsp *grated lemon peel* 5 to 10 mL
> 1/2 cup *whipped cream* 125 mL
> 1 *21-oz can blueberry pie filling or other fruit pie filling* 750 mL
> 6 to 8 *firm strawberries with stems (optional)* 6 to 8

Microwave pie crust according to directions and let cool. In a small bowl, beat together cream cheese, sugar, and lemon peel until light and fluffy. Fold in whipped cream. Spoon into pie crust, spreading evenly. Top evenly with blueberry filling. Cut strawberries into fans to garnish cheesecake. Serves 4 to 6.

Note: To make strawberry fans, select firm berries with stems. Starting at tip, cut thin slices almost to stem. Spread slices to form fan.

REMINISCENCES

This one-dish meal is reminiscent of "shore bakes," when good friends got together and cooked up a potful of the best the sea had to offer. The beauty of this is its quick preparation, delicious taste, and the fact that you can enjoy it while the snow flies or the mosquitoes buzz—in the comfort of your own kitchen. The dessert is decadent.

MENU
Cavendish Seafood Bake
Strawberry Whiz

SEQUENCE
1. Prepare and microwave sauce for strawberry whiz and chill. While sauce is cooking, slice peaches and place in serving dishes.

2. Prepare and microwave Cavendish seafood bake.

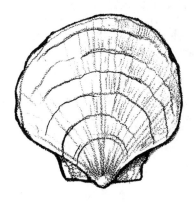

Cavendish Seafood Bake

In Prince Edward Island, there is a new shellfish on the market, bay scallops, which I prefer to clams. If you can't find bay scallops, use littleneck clams or mussels. Serve with fresh rolls and butter.

> 4 *ears corn, shucked and strips of kernels cut into*
>   *2-inch (5-cm) pieces* 4
> 12 *bay scallops, mussels, or littleneck clams in shell* 12
> 2 *8-oz bottles clam juice* 500 mL
> 2 *leeks, thinly sliced* 2
> 2 tbsp *butter* 25 mL
> 1 lb *medium-size shrimp, shelled and deveined* 500 g
> 3/4 lb *large sea scallops, sliced* 375 g
> 2 *cloves garlic, minced* 2
> 1 *7-oz jar roasted sweet red peppers, drained and sliced* 225 mL
> 2 tbsp *lemon juice* 25 mL
> *Spinach leaves*

Assemble corn chunks into ears. Wrap in plastic wrap and microwave at High 6 minutes, rearranging once. Scrub and rinse bay scallops. Place a microwave-safe steamer in a casserole. Add 1/2 cup (125 mL) clam juice. Cover and microwave at High 2 minutes. Add bay scallops, cover, and microwave at High 3 to 3-1/2 minutes or until shells open. Discard any that don't open.

In a 3-qt (3-L) casserole, microwave leeks and butter, covered, at High 3 to 4 minutes. Stir in shrimp, sea scallops, garlic, peppers, lemon juice, and remaining clam juice. Microwave, covered, at High 6 minutes, stirring gently twice. Add bay scallops and liquid and corn and microwave at High until heated through. Add spinach leaves, cover, and serve. Serves 4 to 6.

Strawberry Whiz

This is named for its ease and speed in preparation. As an alternative, serve the sauce over blueberries and ice cream.

> 1 *10-oz pkg frozen strawberries in syrup* 275 g
> *Sugar or orange-flavored liqueur*
> *Fresh or canned peaches, sliced*
> *Ice Cream*

In a loosely covered bowl, defrost strawberries at High 1-1/2 to 2 minutes. Drain, add a small amount of sugar or liqueur, and process in a blender or food processor until puréed. Pour over peaches and ice cream. Serves 4 to 6.

BUSY-DAY BAIL-OUT

Balance this easy-to-prepare pasta casserole with a tossed salad and finish the meal with a delectable sundae.

MENU
Mushroom-Tuna Fettuccine
Vegetables with Mustard Vinaigrette
Kiwi-Raspberry Sundae

SEQUENCE
1. Assemble vegetables in a bag and microwave. While vegetables are cooking, prepare vinaigrette.

2. Prepare ingredients for mushroom-tuna fettuccine while pasta is cooking on stovetop.

3. While pasta is draining, prepare and microwave kiwi-raspberry sauce.

4. Assemble fettuccine casserole and microwave. While cooking fettuccine, arrange vegetables on a serving platter and top with mustard vinaigrette.

Mushroom-Tuna Fettuccine

This dish, suitable for any kind of pasta, is nutritional and economical. We use low-calorie, low-sodium soup and water instead of milk unless serving company.

3 cups *cooked spinach fettuccine* 750 mL
1 *10-oz can cream of mushroom soup* 284 mL
1/2 cup *milk* 125 mL
1 cup *grated Cheddar cheese* 250 mL
1 tbsp *grated Parmesan cheese (optional)* 15 mL
1 *6-1/2-oz can tuna* 184 g
1 cup *sliced fresh mushrooms* 250 mL
1/3 cup *finely chopped onion* 75 mL
1/3 cup *finely chopped celery* 75 mL

Cook fettuccine on stovetop according to directions. Meanwhile, in a 2-qt (2-L) casserole, combine soup, milk, half of Cheddar, and Parmesan until well blended. Add drained pasta, tuna, mushrooms, onion, and celery, mixing gently to not break up tuna. Cover and microwave at High 5 minutes. Stir or toss gently to mix, drawing out center to sides of casserole. Microwave, uncovered, at High 3 more minutes. Sprinkle with remaining Cheddar and microwave at Medium (50%) until cheese melts. Serves 4 to 6.

Note: Any type of pasta works well. If using long pasta, such as spaghetti or fettuccine, break or cut into short lengths.

Variation: To make shrimp fettuccine, substitute 1 10-oz (284-mL) can shrimp bisque for cream of mushroom soup, 1 6-1/2-oz (184-g) can shrimp for tuna, and 1 cup (250 mL) frozen peas or mixed vegetables for fresh mushrooms. Make sure vegetables are cooked before adding remaining Cheddar.

Vegetables with Mustard Vinaigrette

When preparing this dish, be sure to use pint-size (500-mL) zip-lock bags that are microwave safe.

1 cup *small broccoli florets* 250 mL
1 cup *small cauliflower florets* 250 mL
1 cup *1/4-inch (1-cm) rounds carrots,*
    yellow summer squash, or zucchini 250 mL
1 cup *2-inch green beans* 250 mL
1 cup *trimmed snow peas* 250 mL
Mustard Vinaigrette:
2 tbsp *red wine vinegar* 25 mL
2 tbsp *Dijon mustard* 25 mL
1/2 tsp *minced garlic* 2 mL
1/2 tsp *sugar* 2 mL
1/2 tsp *salt* 2 mL
1/2 cup *olive oil* 125 mL

Place each vegetable in a separate plastic bag. Partially close bags, leaving an opening for steam to escape. Arrange in a circle on oven floor, making sure bags do not touch. Microwave at High 5 to 10 minutes or until vegetables are tender-crisp; cooking times will vary.

Check after 5 minutes and rearrange bags. Remove each bag from oven as vegetable is done (snow peas, 5 minutes; broccoli and summer squash, 7 minutes; cauliflower and green beans, 9 minutes; and carrots, 10 minutes). Immediately run bags under cold water to stop cooking process. Drain any cooking liquid through opening in top.

Open bags and arrange vegetables on a serving platter. In a small bowl, whisk together all vinaigrette ingredients except olive oil. Whisk in olive oil. Pour vinaigrette over warm vegetables. Serves 6.

Kiwi-Raspberry Sundae

Apple jelly makes a great base for a light sauce.

> 10 oz *apple jelly* 300 mL
> 3 *kiwi, peeled and quartered* 3
> 1 cup *fresh raspberries* 250 mL
> *Ice cream or cake*
> *Sliced kiwi, raspberries, or mint leaves for garnish*

Remove lid from jar of jelly and place jar on a plate. Microwave, uncovered, at High 3 minutes or until jelly melts. Using potholders, carefully remove jar from oven. Pour jelly into a blender or food processor. Drop in kiwi and process until mixture is puréed. Transfer to serving bowl and gently stir in berries. Pour sauce over ice cream or cake and garnish with sliced kiwi, raspberries, or mint leaves.

Variations: Substitute any of the following combinations for kiwi and raspberries: strawberries and orange zest, cantaloupe and watermelon, or pineapple chunks and a dash of grenadine. Use varying amounts to taste. For a Middle-Eastern twist, add 1 tbsp (15 mL) rose water or orange-flower water to apple jelly after cooking. Serve over lemon and tangerine wedges or a fruit sherbet.

A TASTE OF SCANDINAVIA

The salad is a meal in itself and, served with fresh bread and butter, is just right for a hot summer day; the cheesecake is the perfect finishing touch. Because the whole meal is prepared in advance, there is no need for sequencing.

MENU
Scandinavian Poached-Fish Salad
Mocha-Almond Cheesecake

Scandinavian Poached-Fish Salad

2 *medium-size red potatoes, thinly sliced* 2
2 tbsp *water* 25 mL
12 oz *firm cod fillets or other lean fish, cut into*
   1-1/2-inch (3.5-cm) chunks 375 g
2 cups *torn iceberg lettuce* 500 mL
2 cups *torn romaine lettuce* 500 mL
1 cup *diced pickled beets* 250 mL
1 *apple, cut into wedges* 1
Dressing:
1/2 cup *low-fat plain yogurt* 125 mL
1 tbsp *finely chopped red onion* 15 mL
1 tbsp *salt-free catsup* 15 mL
1 tbsp *sweet relish* 15 mL
Seasoning:
2 *slices red onion* 2
2 tbsp *white vinegar* 25 mL
1/8 tsp *whole allspice* 0.5 mL
1/8 tsp *whole cloves* 0.5 mL
1/8 tsp *whole peppercorns* 0.5 mL
1 tbsp *water* 15 mL

In a mixing bowl, blend all dressing ingredients. Cover and chill. Place potatoes in a 1-qt (1-L) casserole. Sprinkle with 2 tbsp (25 mL) water. Cover and microwave at High 5 to 7 minutes or until tender, stirring once. Set aside.

Meanwhile, in a 2-qt (2-L) casserole, combine all seasoning ingredients. Stir in fish. Cover and microwave at High 3-1/2 to 6 minutes or until fish flakes easily, stirring once. Let stand, covered, 3 minutes. Drain and chill 1-1/2 hours. Arrange lettuce on a large platter. Place fish in center and surround with beets, potato slices, and apple wedges. Pour dressing over salad.

Mocha-Almond Cheesecake

The almonds in the crust add a special touch to this rich, flavorful cheesecake.

> **Crust:**
> 1 cup *graham-wafer crumbs* 250 mL
> 1/4 cup *ground almonds* 50 mL
> 1/4 cup *butter* 50 mL
> **Filling:**
> 3 4-1/2-oz *pkg cream cheese, softened* 3
> 1/3 cup *sugar* 75 mL
> 2 *eggs* 2
> 1/2 cup *sour cream* 125 mL
> 3 tbsp *coffee liqueur* 50 mL
> 1 sq *semisweet chocolate, finely chopped or grated* 30 g
> *Almond slices for garnish (optional)*

Prepare crust. In a bowl, combine crumbs and ground almonds. Place butter in a 9-inch (22.5-cm) pie plate. Microwave, uncovered, at High 30 seconds or until butter is melted. Add to crumb mixture and mix well. Press crust onto bottom and sides of pie plate. Microwave at Medium-High (70%) 1-1/2 minutes.

Prepare filling. In a mixing bowl or in a food processor fitted with metal blade, combine cream cheese, sugar, eggs, sour cream, and liqueur. Beat or process until smooth. Pour into crust and sprinkle chocolate over top.

Place pie plate on a 1-inch (2.5-cm) high rack. Microwave at Medium-High (70%) 8 minutes or until set around edges and almost set in center. Cool, then chill. Sprinkle with almond slices if desired.

PASTA PERFECT

The fusilli, tomatoes, and roasted green peppers with basil aioli goes well with a simple fish-and-spinach dish. This light meal is rounded out with a comforting bread pudding.

MENU
Spinach Roll-ups
Fusilli, Tomatoes, and Roasted Green Peppers with Basil Aioli
Pineapple-Blueberry Bread Pudding with Custard Sauce

SEQUENCE
1. Prepare and microwave pineapple-blueberry bread pudding. While cooking, assemble ingredients for custard sauce.

2. Microwave custard sauce if desired and serve cold or microwave after eating main course and serve warm.

3. Prepare and microwave fusilli dish. Set aside. Meanwhile, prepare and microwave spinach roll-ups.

Spinach Roll-ups

1/2 cup *thinly sliced leek* 125 mL
2 tbsp *butter* 25 mL
1 *10-oz pkg frozen spinach, defrosted* 300 g
4 *thin white-fish fillets* 4
Finely grated peel 1 lemon
2 tbsp *freshly squeezed lemon juice* 25 mL
Salt to taste
Freshly ground pepper to taste

Place leek and butter in a pie plate. Microwave, covered, at High 5 minutes. Set aside. Place spinach in a sieve and gently press out excess water. Pat dry. Spread each fillet with 1/4 of spinach, then leek, lemon peel, and juice. Sprinkle with salt and pepper. Roll up each fillet, starting at narrow end. Place fillets, seam side down, near dish edge. Microwave, uncovered, at High 5 minutes or until fish flakes easily with a fork.

Note: Try to get thin fish fillets that are about same size and of uniform thickness.

Fusilli, Tomatoes, and Roasted Green Peppers with Basil Aioli

This California recipe can be served at once or covered and set aside for 30 minutes at room temperature before serving, giving lots of time to prepare the rest of a meal.

1 lb *fusilli pasta* 500 g
2 tbsp *olive oil* 25 mL
2 *large green peppers* 2
4 *large cloves garlic, unpeeled* 4
1 cup *mayonnaise* 250 mL
3 tbsp *minced fresh basil* 50 mL
Dash *sugar* Dash
Dash *cayenne pepper* Dash
1/4 tsp *black pepper* 1 mL
Salt
12 *cherry tomatoes, halved or quartered* 12

In a large pot, cook fusilli on stovetop according to package directions and drain well. In a large serving bowl, toss pasta with olive oil and set aside.

Place green peppers in a plastic bag, tie ends, and set on oven floor. Microwave at High 3 to 4 minutes. Turn bag over and rotate a half-turn. Wrap garlic in paper towel and place in oven beside peppers. Microwave at High 3 to 4 minutes or until peppers are slightly tender and garlic is very tender. Let peppers and garlic stand 5 minutes.

Remove peppers from bag and cool under cold water. Peel, seed, pat dry on paper towel, and dice. Squeeze garlic from skins into a food processor. Add mayonnaise, basil, sugar, and cayenne and pulse 6 to 8 times or until creamy. Add 3/4 cup (175 mL) garlic mixture to pasta, along with diced green peppers. Add black pepper and salt, tossing well. Add tomatoes and toss gently. If pasta seems dry, add remaining garlic mixture and toss gently.

Pineapple-Blueberry Bread Pudding with Custard Sauce

This recipe, from the Egg Marketing Agency, is a sign of the comeback of comfort food. Quick to prepare, the pudding is "as inviting as grandma's kitchen."

> 1 14-oz can crushed pineapple in juice 389 mL
> 6 slices bread, cubed 6
> 4 eggs 4
> 1/3 cup packed brown sugar 75 mL
> 1 cup frozen unsweetened blueberries 75 mL
> **Custard Sauce:**
> 1/4 cup granulated sugar 50 mL
> 1-1/2 tsp cornstarch 7 mL
> 1-1/2 cups milk 375 mL
> 2 eggs, beaten 2
> 1/2 tsp vanilla 2 mL

Drain pineapple well, reserving 1/2 cup (125 mL) juice. Set aside. Place bread cubes in greased 6-cup (1.5-L) ring mold. In a bowl, beat together 4 eggs and brown sugar. Stir in pineapple and reserved juice. Pour mixture over bread. Sprinkle blueberries evenly over top. Cover loosely with wax paper and microwave at Medium-High (70%) 8 minutes or until set. Let stand, covered, 10 minutes.

Meanwhile, prepare custard sauce. In a 4-cup (1-L) measure, combine granulated sugar and cornstarch. Gradually stir in milk. Microwave, uncovered, at High 4 minutes or until mixture boils and thickens, stirring every 2 minutes. Whisk about 1/3 of hot mixture into 2 beaten eggs. Add egg mixture to remaining cornstarch mixture and blend well. Microwave at Medium-High (70%) 30 seconds or *just* until thickened. Stir in vanilla. Serve warm or cold over bread pudding. Serves 6.

WEST-COAST GOURMET

This menu is wonderful for entertaining because so much of the work can be done ahead of time. I can never see the point of inviting guests, then spending all of one's time in the kitchen. All too often the cook is drying his or her hands on a tea towel as guests are gathering their things to leave. If desired, to round out this meal, serve a crisp green salad and a loaf of whole-grain or other gourmet bread that can be sliced at the table. If you have true oyster lovers in your midst, serve a few on the half-shell with lemon and Tabasco.

MENU
Oysters and Wild Rice
Gourmet Red-Pepper Salad
Peaches Romanoff

SEQUENCE
1.   Long before company arrives, prepare gourmet red-pepper salad and Peaches Romanoff up to serving stage.

2.   Assemble ingredients for oysters and wild rice, prepare, and microwave.

3.   1-1/2 hours before dining, soak wild rice. Drain after 1 hour.

4.   Prepare oysters and wild rice. When removed from oven, seat guests at table.

Oysters and Wild Rice

This Vancouver recipe is great with east-coast Malpeque oysters.

2/3 cup *wild rice* 175 mL
2 cups *boiling water* 500 mL
2 tbsp *butter* 25 mL
1 *small onion, chopped* 1
1/2 cup *chopped mushrooms* 125 mL
2 tbsp *chopped parsley* 25 mL
1 tsp *dried chervil* 5 mL
Salt and pepper to taste
1 pt *shucked oysters, drained* 500 mL
2 tbsp *melted butter* 25 mL
1/2 cup *dry white wine* 125 mL
Paprika

Wash rice in cold water and drain. Stir into boiling water in a saucepan and boil only 5 minutes. Remove from heat and let rice soak in same water, covered, 1 hour. Drain, rinse, and drain again well.

In a medium-size bowl, microwave butter, uncovered, at High 45 seconds. Add onion, mushrooms, and parsley; mix. Season with chervil, salt, and pepper, blending well. Microwave at High 1-1/2 to 2 minutes or until onion is transparent. Add rice and mix well.

Divide rice mixture among 4 greased soufflé dishes. Spread mixture evenly over bottoms. Place oysters on top of rice mixture. Spoon 1 tsp (5 mL) melted butter over each dish of oysters, then 2 tbsp (25 mL) wine. Cover each with plastic wrap, leaving a vent. Arrange dishes in a square in oven. Microwave at High 8 minutes, rotating dishes a half-turn twice. Edges of oysters should curl. Sprinkle with paprika.

Gourmet Red-Pepper Salad

6 *green onions* 6
3 *sweet red peppers, cored, seeded, and cut into*
    1/4-inch (5-mm) wide strips 3
3 *sweet yellow or green peppers, cut same as red* 3
2 tbsp *olive oil* 25 mL
2 tbsp *water* 25 mL
1 *clove garlic, smashed, peeled, and finely chopped* 1
1 tsp *capers, drained and coarsely chopped* 5 mL
1 tsp *fresh thyme leaves or 1/4 tsp (1 mL) dried* 5 mL
1/4 tsp *coarse (kosher) salt* 1 mL
1/8 tsp *pepper* 1 mL
1 tbsp *white wine vinegar* 15 mL

Cut white parts of green onions into 2-inch (5-cm) pieces. Reserve green parts. Cut white pieces lengthwise in half or quarters for uniform thickness. Place red peppers in bottom of a 2-qt (2-L) soufflé dish. Sprinkle white parts of onion around perimeter of dish. Top with yellow peppers.

In a small measure, combine olive oil, water, garlic, capers, thyme, salt, and pepper, mixing well. Pour over peppers. Cover dish tightly with plastic wrap. Microwave at High 6 to 8 minutes or until peppers reach desired tenderness. Remove from oven and pierce plastic wrap with tip of knife to release steam. Carefully remove plastic wrap. Thinly slice enough reserved green onion to make 1/2 cup (125 mL). Add to peppers, along with vinegar; toss to coat peppers. Serve warm or chilled.

Peaches Romanoff

Peaches microwave well because they are a firm, fragrant fruit. However, time them and tend to them carefully so that they retain their shape and full flavor. Not all peach varieties microwave equally well: the plumper, firmer, fresher, and more aromatic the peach, the better.

1/2 cup *sugar* 125 mL
1/2 cup *freshly squeezed orange juice* 125 mL
1/4 cup *water* 50 mL
1/4 cup *orange liqueur* 50 mL
4 *large firm, ripe peaches* 4
2 tbsp *lemon juice* 25 mL
4 *small scoops strawberry ice cream* 4
1 cup *whipping cream, whipped until stiff* 250 mL
4 tsp *slivered candied orange zest or candied ginger* 20 mL

In a shallow 2-inch (5-cm) deep 9-inch (22.5-cm) casserole, combine sugar, orange juice, water, and liqueur. Cover with wax paper and microwave at High 2 to 3 minutes or until mixture boils and sugar dissolves, stirring halfway through.

Meanwhile, peel, halve, and pit peaches. Roll in lemon juice to keep from darkening. Stir sugar-orange mixture, then arrange peaches, hollow-sides-up and not touching, in casserole. Cover with plastic wrap, leaving a vent, or lid and microwave at High 3 to 4 minutes, turning peaches over and rotating casserole a half-turn halfway through. (Don't overcook, as peaches continue cooking while cooling.) Cool peaches, covered, in syrup until they reach room temperature. Turn occasionally. Chill, covered, several hours.

Serve in 4 goblets. Spoon 2 spoonfuls of syrup into each goblet. Sandwich 2 peach halves together with 1 scoop ice cream in center and place 1 sandwich in each goblet. Top with whipped cream, then zest. Pass around any remaining syrup in a small jug.

BUNCH FOR LUNCH

Creamy mussel soup, fresh bread and butter, a crisp salad, and a decadent dessert is perfect weekend lunch fare. The soup requires a fair amount of hands-on time, so decide whether you want to prepare the dessert ahead of time and serve it at room temperature or while the table is being cleared and the coffee being made.

MENU
Creamy Mussel Soup
Orange Clouds

SEQUENCE
1. Prepare and microwave orange clouds to stage of adding meringue.

2. Prepare and microwave creamy mussel soup.

3. Enjoy soup.

4. Prepare meringue and complete orange clouds.

Creamy Mussel Soup

Serve this garnished with a slice of hard-boiled egg and a sprinkle of paprika. There is plenty for lunch for four or as an appetizer for a dinner party of eight. If we have a mussel "feed" one night, we use the leftovers in this soup the next day.

4 lb *mussels, cleaned (about 50)* 2 kg
3 tbsp *butter* 50 mL
3 tbsp *chopped leek (white part only)* 50 mL
1 tbsp *fennel seeds, well crushed* 15 mL
1/4 tsp *white pepper* 1 mL
Dash *salt (optional)* Dash
1 *egg yolk* 1
1 tbsp *cornstarch* 15 mL
1/2 cup *vermouth* 125 mL
1 cup *milk* 250 mL
1/2 cup *heavy cream* 125 mL
1 *hard-boiled egg, sliced, for garnish* 1
Paprika for garnish

Divide mussels into thirds. In a pie plate, microwave each third, uncovered, at High 1-1/2 minutes. Discard any that do not open. Remove meat from mussels and set aside.

In a large bowl, microwave butter, uncovered, at High 45 seconds. Add leek, fennel seeds, pepper, and salt. Microwave at High 1-1/2 minutes.

In a small bowl, beat egg yolk with cornstarch. Add vermouth gradually, blending well. Stir egg mixture into leek mixture. Microwave, uncovered, at High 1 minute, stirring once. Add milk and cream gradually, blending well. Microwave at High 4 minutes, stirring twice. Add mussels. Microwave, covered, at High 1-1/2 minutes or until soup is heated through. Garnish with a slice of hard-boiled egg and paprika. Serves 4 to 8.

Note: If desired, increase amount of fennel seeds by 1 tsp (5 mL).

Orange Clouds

One evening, a friend and I were thumbing through magazines and recipe books and cooking whatever struck our fancy. We found this in a magazine, made it, and ate the whole thing while sipping coffee laced with Grand Marnier. If dinner requires a lot of attention, make this ahead of time and serve cool. For a heavenly experience, serve warm with coffee or hot chocolate.

    2 tbsp *cornstarch* 25 mL
    2 cups *orange juice* 500 mL
    2 tbsp *honey* 25 mL
    1 *cinnamon stick* 1
    2 *egg whites* 2
    1/4 tsp *cream of tartar* 1 mL
    3 tbsp *sugar* 50 mL
    1 tsp *orange zest* 5 mL

Place cornstarch in a 4-cup (1-L) measure and slowly stir in orange juice until smooth. Mix in honey and drop in cinnamon stick. Microwave, uncovered, at High 4-1/2 to 5-1/2 minutes, stirring once. It should boil. Pour into an 8-inch (20-cm) serving dish and remove cinnamon stick.

In medium-size bowl, beat together egg whites and cream of tartar until soft peaks form. Gradually beat in sugar until stiff, but not dry, peaks form. Spoon mounds of meringue onto orange sauce to make clouds and sprinkle with zest. Microwave, uncovered, at High, 1-1/2 to 2 minutes or until meringue is set, rotating dish once halfway through cooking.

FAMILY FAVORITE

We like to round out this meal with steamed rice. You may wish to begin with a salad or an appetizer. If you don't like green beans, serve the sole fillets with squash topped with butter and pepper.

MENU
Sole Fillets with Mushroom-Tomato Sauce
Green Beans Italiano or Squash
Pecan Torte

SEQUENCE
1. Prepare pecan torte and microwave. While torte is cooking, assemble ingredients for sole fillets, mushroom-tomato sauce, and Green Beans Italiano or squash.

2. Microwave green beans or squash. Meanwhile, prepare sole fillets.

3. Remove green beans or squash from oven and microwave sole fillets. Meanwhile, complete green beans or squash and transfer to hot plates and cover.

4. When fish is done, prepare and microwave mushroom-tomato sauce.

Sole Fillets with Mushroom-Tomato Sauce

I cut this recipe out of a magazine long before I bought my microwave and have always been glad I saved it. The quick cream sauce makes a dish that's fancy enough for company. Serve with rice steamed on the stovetop.

1 lb *sole fillets* 500 g
1 cup *sliced mushrooms* 250 mL
1 *tomato, peeled, seeded, and chopped* 1
2 tbsp *chopped green onion* 25 mL
1/4 cup *dry white wine* 50 mL
1/2 cup *whipping cream* 125 mL
1 tbsp *cornstarch* 15 mL
1 tsp *lemon juice* 5 mL
Pinch *cayenne pepper* Pinch
Salt and pepper to taste
2 tbsp *chopped fresh parsley* 25 mL

Arrange sole fillets in spoke fashion on a pie plate, folding over at thin ends. Top with mushrooms, tomato, and green onion. Drizzle with wine. Cover with plastic wrap, leaving a vent, and microwave at High 3 to 5 minutes or until fish is opaque. Turn dish once during cooking. Drain cooking juices and set aside. Let stand, covered, 2 minutes.

In a 2-cup (500-mL) measure, blend together cream and cornstarch; stir in reserved juices. Microwave, uncovered, at High 1 to 1-1/2 minutes or until thickened, whisking once. Stir in lemon juice, cayenne, salt, and pepper. Pour over fish. Top with parsley.

Green Beans Italiano

1-1/2 tbsp *butter* 25 mL
1 *clove garlic, finely chopped* 1
1 lb *fresh green beans, trimmed* 500 g
1/4 tsp *leaf oregano, crumbled* 1 mL
2 tbsp *water* 25 mL
Freshly ground pepper to taste
4 tsp *grated Parmesan cheese* 20 mL
Lemon wedges

Place butter and garlic in a 1-1/2-qt (1.5-L) casserole. Microwave, uncovered, at High 1 minute. Mix in beans, oregano, water, and pepper. Cover and microwave at High 8 to 12 minutes or until beans are tender, stirring after 5 minutes. Sprinkle with Parmesan cheese and garnish with lemon wedges. Squeeze juice over to eat.

Squash

---

1 *2-1/2- to 3-lb squash* 1.25 to 1.5 kg
Butter
Pepper

With a sharp knife, make 4 to 6 incisions through peel of squash to allow steam to escape. Place on a rack or inverted saucer and microwave at High 6 to 10 minutes, depending on size. Using potholders, remove squash from oven. Let stand 10 to 15 minutes, then cut in half. Gently remove seeds and fiber and discard. Scoop out pulp or mash in shell. (For spaghetti squash, use two forks to shred pulp into strands.) Before serving, cover with wax paper and microwave at High 4 to 5 minutes. Dot with butter, sprinkle with pepper, and serve.

Note: If desired, use maple syrup or brown sugar instead of butter and pepper.

Pecan Torte

This recipe comes from Florida, where you can indulge in wonderful fresh pecans.

14 *graham crackers* 14
1 cup *sugar* 250 mL
1 tsp *baking powder* 5 mL
1/2 tsp *salt* 2 mL
3 *egg yolks* 3
3 *egg whites, beaten stiff* 3
1 tsp *vanilla* 5 mL
3/4 cup *pecans, chopped* 175 mL
Whipped cream or ice cream
Whole pecans for garnish

Crush graham crackers. In a bowl, mix together graham-cracker crumbs and dry ingredients. Add egg yolks and fold in beaten egg whites. Add vanilla and chopped nuts. Microwave on Bake (70%) 8 to 10 minutes. Let stand 5 minutes. Garnish with chopped pecans and serve with whipped cream or ice cream. Serves 8.

EARTH, SEA, AND VINE

Teaming an elegant, light dessert with halibut and root vegetables keeps people at the table. The garlic sauce complements both the fish and the vegetables, and the grape dessert is perfect for munching on while enjoying good conversation.

MENU
Halibut Steaks
One-Dish Root Medley
Garlic Sauce
Grapes with Tarragon

SEQUENCE
1.   At least 2-1/2 hours before mealtime, prepare grapes with tarragon. Chill until served.

2.   Assemble ingredients for one-dish root medley.

3.   Prepare and microwave halibut steaks. While cooking halibut steaks, prepare garlic sauce.

4.   When halibut steaks are done, let stand, covered. Meanwhile, microwave root medley.

5.   As root medley finishes cooking, place halibut steaks on a hot serving plate. Take all to table.

Halibut Steaks

> *2 halibut steaks, about 1 inch (2.5 cm) thick*
>   *(about 1/2 lb/250 g each) 2*
> *2 green onions, sliced 2*
> *Lemon juice or white wine*

Place halibut fillets on a pie plate or platter, top with green onion, and drizzle with lemon juice or white wine. Cover with plastic wrap, leaving a vent. Microwave at High 5 to 7 minutes. Let stand 2 to 3 minutes. To serve, transfer to a hot dish.

One-Dish Root Medley

Although we've used root vegetables as the main ingredients, you can substitute any vegetables you wish. But make sure they are cooked before serving.

> 4 *small new potatoes, scrubbed*
>   *and halved (about 1/2 lb/250 g)* 4
> 4 *fresh beets, scrubbed and quartered (about 1 lb/500 g)* 4
> 1 *turnip, scrubbed and cut into small wedges*
>   *or sticks (about 3/4 lb/350 g)* 1
> 4 *cherry tomatoes* 4
> 1/2 lb *green beans, halved lengthwise* 250 g
> *Salt and pepper to taste*

Arrange potatoes, beets, and turnip on outside of a large pie plate. Form inner ring with green beans, leaving a space in middle. Prick cherry tomatoes with a toothpick a few times and place in center. (If you prefer them uncooked, add before serving.) Cover dish tightly with plastic wrap and microwave at High 5 to 8 minutes or until medley is cooked as desired. Season with salt and pepper and serve with garlic sauce on the side.

Garlic Sauce

This mayonnaise-style sauce is also known as *aioli*. It adds character to simply prepared fish and vegetables.

> 1 *egg* 1
> 1 tbsp *white wine vinegar or lemon juice* 15 mL
> 1 tsp *salt* 5 mL
> 3/4 cup *olive oil* 175 mL
> 3/4 cup *corn or safflower oil* 175 mL
> 1 *large or 2 small cloves garlic, peeled* 1
> *Salt to taste*
> 1/4 tsp *freshly ground pepper* 1 mL
> *Vinegar to taste (optional)*

Place egg, vinegar, and salt in a food processor fitted with metal blade. Cover and process 2 to 3 seconds or until well blended. With motor still running, gradually add oils through feed tube. Sauce should thicken. Drop in garlic and continue processing until smooth. Taste and season with salt, pepper, and/or vinegar. Makes about 1-1/2 cups (375 mL).

Note: Sauce can be stored in refrigerator for up to 1 week.

Grapes with Tarragon

Grapes and tarragon are a delightful combination when poached with anise-flavored liqueur. Cantaloupe is also delicious with fresh tarragon. To serve four, make two batches.

> 1 cup *water* 250 mL
> 1/4 cup *sugar* 50 mL
> 1 tbsp *Pernod or Ricard* 15 mL
> 3 *sprigs fresh tarragon, plus a few sprigs for garnish* 3
> 2 *bunches seedless red grapes (about 1/2 lb/250 g each)* 2

In a small bowl or measure, combine water, sugar, and liqueur. Microwave, uncovered, at High 3 minutes or until sugar dissolves. Mix well, then pour into a pie plate. Add grapes and tarragon sprigs. Cover with plastic wrap and seal tightly. Microwave at High 2 minutes, turn grapes over, and microwave 2 more minutes. Let cool to room temperature, then refrigerate at least 2 hours or until cold. Remove tarragon sprigs. Garnish grapes with fresh tarragon and serve with poaching liquid. Serves 2.

OLD-TIME NEW ENGLAND SUPPER

Travelling through Maine, we asked several elderly people what their favorite traditional meal was. The most common answer was baked beans with salt pork, reminding us of the days in logging camps when beans simmered on the woodstove all day. Using a microwave, the cooking time is reduced drastically, but the beans still have to be prepared the same way. We've developed a new mackerel recipe as an alternative to the old-fashioned pan-frying method.

MENU
Mackerel with Dark Sauce
Old-Time Baked Beans
Rice Pudding

SEQUENCE
1.   The day before, soak beans according to directions on package.

2.   Well before mealtime, prepare and microwave rice pudding.

3.   An hour before eating, finish preparing old-time baked beans according to recipe, and microwave. While beans are cooking, prepare mackerel with dark sauce.

4.   While beans are standing, microwave mackerel with dark sauce.

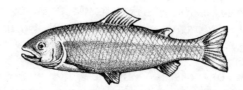

Mackerel with Dark Sauce

The sweet-and-sour sauce used to cook these fillets is an excellent marinade for barbecuing, particularly for fatty fish like mackerel. Naturally, as it is a family standby, we adapted it for the microwave when rain forced a barbecue indoors.

4 *mackerel fillets* 4
Dark Sauce:
1/2 cup *soy sauce* 125 mL
1/4 cup *catsup* 50 mL
1/4 cup *chopped parsley* 50 mL
1/2 cup *orange juice* 125 mL
2 *cloves garlic, minced* 2
2 tbsp *lemon juice* 25 mL
1/4 tsp *pepper* 1 mL

Prepare sauce by thoroughly mixing together all ingredients. Chill in a glass container until ready to use. Gently wash mackerel fillets. Place microwave bag in a pie plate, then arrange fillets in a circle in bag so that thickest part is toward outside of pie plate. Drizzle with sauce. Tie bag using tie provided and following directions for bag. Marinate for 15 minutes to 2 hours.

Microwave at High 5 to 8 minutes, depending on size of fillets. Leave in cooking bag until ready to serve. To serve, carefully open bag by cutting below tie with scissors. (Watch out for steam.) Ease fillets and sauce into pie plate. Spoon sauce over fillets.

Note: Sauce is strong, so just spoon a little over fillets. Unused sauce can be refrigerated for up to 2 weeks.

Old-Time Baked Beans

Using the microwave for this traditional east-coast dish reduces cooking time by 50%, reduces the risk of boiling over and scorched pots and, in summer, has the added benefit of a cool kitchen.

1 *medium-size yellow onion, minced* 1
1/4 lb *lean salt pork, cut into 1/4-inch (3-mm) cubes* 125 g
5 to 5-1/2 cups *cooked navy or pea beans* 1.25 to 1.375 L
Bean liquid from cooking, plus enough water to total
    3/4 to 1 cup (175 to 250 mL)
1/3 cup *dark brown sugar, packed* 75 mL
1/4 cup *dark molasses* 50 mL
2 tbsp *Worcestershire Sauce* 25 mL
1 tbsp *dry mustard* 15 mL
1/4 tsp *black pepper* 1 mL
Salt to taste

In a 4- or 5-qt (4- or 5-L) casserole, combine onion and salt pork. Cover with paper towel and microwave at High 4 minutes, stirring halfway through. Stir in beans, 3/4 cup (175 mL) bean liquid, and water, brown sugar, molasses, Worcestershire, mustard, and pepper. Cover with wax paper and microwave at High 9 to 10 minutes or until gently bubbling, stirring halfway through.

Reduce power to Medium (50%) and microwave, covered with a tight lid, 30 to 35 minutes, stirring carefully halfway through. When stirring, check liquid and add remaining bean liquid and water if beans seem dry. When done, stir again and let stand, covered, 10 minutes. Season with salt. Serves 6.

Note: In a microwave of less than 600 watts, increase cooking time by 15%. The following are other rules to remember:

1. Use a casserole at least twice the size of volume of ingredients.

2. Cover with a tight lid to keep beans from drying. Plastic wrap may split during long cooking.

3. Do not add salt until after cooking. Salt can toughen beans.

4. Do not hurry beans along by keeping power at High. They will toughen and dry. Once bean liquid has come to a boil, reduce power to Medium (50%) so beans will absorb liquid slowly and will soften.

5. Make sure beans are tender before removing from microwave. Although they continue to absorb liquid when standing, they won't become any more tender. If beans aren't
tender at end of recommended cooking time, continue microwaving in 5-minute increments, stirring after each. Some
beans take longer than others.

Rice Pudding

2 cups *milk* 500 mL
2 *eggs, lightly beaten* 2
1/2 cup *sugar* 125 mL
1 tsp *vanilla* 5 mL
1/4 tsp *ground cinnamon* 1 mL
1/8 tsp *grated nutmeg* 0.5 mL
1/2 cup *quick-cooking rice* 125 mL
1/2 cup *raisins* 125 mL
2 tsp *grated lemon rind* 10 mL

Pour milk into a 4-cup (1-L) glass measure. Microwave, uncovered, at High 3 minutes or until hot (do not boil). Set aside.

In a 1-1/2-qt (1.5-L) casserole, combine eggs, sugar, vanilla,
cinnamon, and nutmeg. Mix well. Stir in rice, raisins, lemon rind,
and hot milk.

Set casserole in a slightly larger baking dish that contains 1 inch
(2.5 cm) hot water. Microwave, uncovered, at High 2 minutes,
then switch setting to Low/Defrost and microwave 8 more minutes. Stir, moving cooked portion to center. Sprinkle top with
additional grated nutmeg if desired. Microwave at Low/Defrost
8 to 12 more minutes or until knife inserted in center comes out
clean. Let stand, uncovered, until cool. Refrigerate until ready to
serve. Serve chilled or warm. Serves 4 to 6.

Meals for up to Eight

The following menus are wonderful when company is coming for dinner. Because microwaved food tends to cool quickly, I suggest investing in a warming tray. Place dishes on the tray as they come out of the microwave, and everyone will enjoy a hot meal. Both menus are fine for a sitdown or buffet meal, making them ideal party fare.

SOME GOOD-"TIME" FARE

In our neighborhood, a gathering for friends, family, or neighbors is often referred to as a "time," signifying good food, good conversation, and good friends. No menu can be more fitting than a scrumptious lobster casserole with lots of "trimmings." The hot fruit compote will delight gourmands if reheated to serve; the holding time allows the flavors to blend.

MENU
Lobster Casserole
Potato Pie
Apple-Cabbage Salad
Hot Fruit Compote

SEQUENCE
1. Prepare apple-cabbage salad several hours before company arrives. Do not add dressing.

2. Prepare hot fruit compote to refrigeration stage. (This can be done up to a day in advance.)

3.   Assemble and microwave potato pie. While cooking, prepare lobster casserole, stir dressing into salad, and place compote alongside prepared peaches and grapes.

4.   Remove potato pie to warming tray to stand. Microwave casserole.

5.   Complete last step of compote while table is being cleared.

Lobster Casserole

This recipe comes from the home economists at the P.E.I. Department of Fisheries. Rice added to the cheese sauce gives it body, and the seafood can be frozen so that it's ready for company.

1/2 lb *fish fillets* 250 g
1/2 lb *scallops* 250 g
1/4 cup *butter* 50 mL
1/4 cup *chopped onion* 50 mL
2 tbsp *chopped green pepper* 25 mL
1/4 cup *flour* 50 mL
2 cups *milk* 500 mL
1/2 tsp *salt* 2 mL
1/4 tsp *pepper* 1 mL
1 tbsp *lemon juice* 15 mL
1 cup *grated Cheddar cheese* 250 mL
1 cup *cooked rice* 250 mL
1 11-oz *can frozen lobster meat, thawed and diced* 320 g
1/2 cup *bread crumbs* 125 mL
1 tbsp *butter, melted* 15 mL
Paprika

Place fish fillets and scallops in a pie plate. Cover with plastic wrap and vent. Microwave at High 3 minutes.

In a 4-cup (1-L) measure, microwave butter, uncovered, at High 1 minute. Add onion and green pepper. Microwave at High 1 to 1-1/2 minutes. Stir in flour. Gradually add milk, stirring until combined. Microwave at High 5 to 6 minutes to thicken, stirring twice. Add salt, pepper, lemon juice, cheese, and rice. Stir well.

Place fillets, scallops, and lobster in a 6-cup (1.5-L) greased casserole. Cover with sauce. Microwave, uncovered, at High 5 minutes and stir.

In a bowl, mix together bread crumbs and butter. Sprinkle on top of casserole. Top with a dash or two of paprika. Microwave, uncovered, at High 3 to 5 minutes. Serves 4 to 6.

Potato Pie

This Prince Edward Island recipe is great to serve for brunch or to a crowd with hearty appetites. It can be made ahead of time and frozen.

Crust:
2-1/2 cups *frozen hash-brown potatoes* 625 mL
Filling:
5 *eggs* 5
1-1/2 cups *grated old Cheddar cheese* 375 mL
1/3 cup *milk* 75 mL
1/2 cup *cottage cheese* 125 mL
1 tsp *salt* 5 mL
2 tbsp *finely chopped onion* 25 mL
1/2 cup *finely chopped green pepper* 125 mL
1/2 cup *chopped mushrooms, optional* 125 mL
1/8 tsp *pepper* 0.5 mL
4 drops *Tabasco Sauce* 4 drops
Topping:
6 *slices bacon, cooked* 6
1/3 cup *crushed Cornflake crumbs* 75 mL

Place bacon in a pie plate and cover with paper towel. Microwave at High 5 to 6 minutes or until well done. In a bowl, crumble bacon and mix with Cornflake crumbs. Assemble pie crust. Press frozen potatoes into a 9-inch (22.5-cm) greased pie plate. Make filling. In a bowl, beat eggs until foamy. Stir in remaining ingredients. Pour into crust. Sprinkle with bacon-crumb mixture.

If oven has a rack, place pie on rack or elevate on inverted saucer. Microwave at High 18 to 20 minutes, turning pie a quarter-turn twice during cooking. Pie will be a little soft in center. Rest, covered with foil, 10 minutes on a wooden board. A knife inserted in center should come out clean. Serves 6 to 8.

Apple-Cabbage Salad

1/4 cup *sugar* 50 mL
1 tbsp *cornstarch* 15 mL
1/2 tsp *celery seeds* 2 mL
1/4 tsp *salt* 1 mL
1/8 tsp *dry mustard* 0.5 mL
3/4 cup *water* 175 mL
3 tbsp *cider vinegar* 50 mL
2 tbsp *mayonnaise or salad dressing* 25 mL
2 tbsp *plain yogurt* 25 mL
6 cups *shredded cabbage* 1.5 L
1 *apple, cored and chopped* 1

Place sugar, cornstarch, celery seeds, salt, and mustard in a bowl. Gradually stir in water and vinegar until mixture is smooth. Microwave, uncovered, at High 2-1/2 to 3 minutes or until mixture boils and thickens slightly, stirring once during cooking. Chill.

About 30 minutes before serving, stir in mayonnaise and yogurt. In a large bowl, mix with cabbage and apple, tossing until coated. Serves 8.

Hot Fruit Compote

Adding the peaches and grapes just before the final heating eliminates the possibility of discoloration or overcooking.

> 1 *14-oz pkg frozen sweetened raspberries, thawed* 425 g
> 2 tbsp *cornstarch* 25 mL
> 1 tbsp *chopped fresh mint leaves*
>   *or 1 tsp (5 mL) dried mint* 15 mL
> 2 tsp *grated orange peel* 10 mL
> 1 tbsp *orange-flavored liqueur* 15 mL
> 2 *19-oz cans peaches, drained and sliced* 1.08 L
> 1 cup *green seedless grapes, halved* 250 mL
> *Fresh mint leaves for garnish*

Drain raspberries over an 8-cup (2-L) casserole; set raspberries aside. Add cornstarch, chopped mint, and orange peel to raspberry juice, mixing well. Microwave, uncovered, at High 3 to 4 minutes or until mixture boils and has thickened, stirring twice. Stir in raspberries and liqueur. Cover and refrigerate overnight.

Before serving, gently fold in peaches and grapes. Microwave, uncovered, at High 3 to 4 minutes or until warm. Garnish with mint leaves. Serves 8.

Note: Compote is also lovely spooned over hard vanilla ice cream or served with old-fashioned lady fingers or angel-food cake. For a stunning dessert, halve an angel-food cake into layers. Spoon on half of compote. Replace top of cake and pour on remaining compote. Serve immediately, with whipped cream if desired.

SPRING MEDLEY

This is a light meal that offers all the delicate tastes of spring. New potatoes, green peas and lettuce, and ever-popular crab cakes are a perfect match. The dessert is a little heavier. That's okay. It's chocolate and orange!

MENU
Crab Cakes with Dill Sauce
Garlic-Lemon New Potatoes
Québécois-Style Green Peas
Chocolate-Orange Zucchini Cake

SEQUENCE
1. Prepare chocolate-orange zucchini cake several hours before cooking rest of meal.

2. Combine all ingredients for crab cakes and put in refrigerator to chill.

3. Prepare garlic-lemon new potatoes and Québécois-style green peas. With 2-tier shelf, microwave together potatoes and peas. To prepare together, place potatoes on bottom rack and microwave at High 6 to 7 minutes, then stir. Place peas on top shelf and microwave at High another 6 to 7 minutes. Stir both at least once during cooking. (Without 2-tier shelf, microwave potatoes, then peas. If necessary, microwave potatoes a few more minutes to reheat.)

4. Meanwhile, assemble crab cakes and mix dill sauce.

5. Remove potatoes and peas to a warming tray.

6. Microwave crab cakes. If doubling recipe for company, cook 1 batch and begin eating. Seconds will then be hot.

Crab Cakes with Dill Sauce

For a variation, use Cornflake crumbs for coating or serve with tomato sauce or vinegar. We like these enough to serve them to a crowd. To serve eight, I cook them in two batches after doubling the recipe.

1 lb *crab meat* 500 g
1/3 cup *whole-wheat bread crumbs,*
    plus more for coating 75 mL
2 tsp *prepared mustard* 10 mL
Few dashes *Worcestershire Sauce* Few dashes
1/2 cup *chopped green onion* 125 mL
1/4 tsp *cayenne or to taste* 1 mL
2 *egg whites* 2
1 tbsp *chopped parsley* 15 mL
1/4 cup *mayonnaise* 50 mL
Freshly ground black pepper
Dill Sauce:
Plain yogurt
Sour Cream
Fresh dill weed, snipped

In a bowl, combine all ingredients except bread crumbs for coating. Chill 30 minutes. Form 8 patties, then coat with bread crumbs and place in a ring around inner rim of a 12-inch (30-cm) pie plate. Cover with paper towel. Microwave at High 5 minutes or until crumbs are golden.

Prepare sauce. Mix equal amounts of plain yogurt and sour cream with snipped fresh dill. Serve with crab cakes.

Serves 4.

Garlic-Lemon New Potatoes

16 *small new potatoes (about 3 lb/1.5 kg)* 16
2 tbsp *olive oil* 25 mL
1 tbsp *lemon juice* 15 mL
1 *small clove garlic, minced* 1
1/4 tsp *freshly ground black pepper* 1 mL
Salt to taste (optional)

Wash potatoes, then cut a band of peel from around center of each. In a bowl, mix together other ingredients. Add potatoes, rolling around until well coated. Cover with plastic wrap, leaving a vent. Microwave at High 12 to 14 minutes, stirring twice during cooking. Remove to warming tray and let stand at least 3 minutes or until tender. Serves 8.

Québécois-Style Green Peas

4 cups *frozen green peas* 1 L
4 cups *loosely packed shredded iceberg lettuce* 1 L
2 tbsp *butter or margarine* 25 mL
1/2 tsp *salt* 2 mL
1/8 tsp *freshly ground black pepper* 0.5 mL

In a bowl, mix together peas and lettuce. Dot with butter and sprinkle with salt and pepper. Cover with plastic wrap, leaving a vent. Microwave at High 6 to 7 minutes or until peas are hot and lettuce is tender-crisp. Stir twice during cooking. Remove to warming tray and let stand at least 2 minutes. Serves 8.

Chocolate-Orange Zucchini Cake

2-1/2 cups *flour* 625 mL
1/2 cup *cocoa* 125 mL
2-1/2 tsp *baking powder* 12 mL
1-1/2 tsp *baking soda* 7 mL
1 tsp *salt* 5 mL
1 tsp *cinnamon* 5 mL
3/4 cup *butter* 175 mL
2 cups *sugar* 500 mL
3 *eggs* 3
2 tsp *grated orange rind* 10 mL
2 tsp *vanilla* 10 mL
2 cups *grated zucchini, drained* 500 mL
1/2 cup *milk* 125 mL
1 cup *nuts, chopped* 250 mL
1/2 cup *orange marmalade* 125 mL

In a medium-size bowl, combine first 6 ingredients. In a large bowl, cream together butter and sugar. Beat in eggs. Stir in orange rind, vanilla, and zucchini. Stir in dry ingredients alternately with milk and nuts. Pour into greased 4-qt (4-L) bundt or tube pan. Microwave, uncovered, at High 13 to 15 minutes or until a toothpick inserted in cake comes out clean. Let stand 10 to 15 minutes. Invert cake on rack to remove. Spread marmalade on warm cake. Serve cool. Serves 10.

Note: Times may vary in different size or different wattage ovens. Always test at shortest time if done.

Snacks & Party Fare

The microwave comes into its own when you have company. Whether it's a crowd watching a game, kids having a party, a couple for cards, or unexpected guests, it gets you out of the kitchen and where the action is, especially if you have on hand some staples that can be made quickly into tasty snacks.

Hot-Pepper Mushrooms

These are delicious. The moisture in the mushroom caps create a steaming effect. Serve alone or use them to surround a meal of fish fillets or steaks. Sprinkle both with hot-pepper sauce.

> *Butter or margarine*
> *Mushroom caps*
> *Hot-pepper sauce*

Rub a small amount of butter on bottom of a plate or dish. Place mushroom caps, open side up, in circles with smallest to center. Sprinkle a few drops of hot-pepper sauce in each. Cover with plastic wrap, leaving a vent. Microwave at High 4 to 8 minutes, depending on number and size of mushrooms.

Note: The larger the mushroom cap, the longer the cooking time.

Olé Mexican Fondue

This spicy fondue is a sure hit when served with shrimp, scallops, and vegetables suitable for dipping. Choose mild, medium, or hot salsa according to taste.

> *Medium-size shrimp and scallops, poached*
> *Vegetables suitable for dipping*
> **Dip:**
> 2 tbsp *butter* 25 mL
> 3 tbsp *flour* 50 mL
> 1/3 cup *finely chopped onion* 75 mL
> 1/2 tsp *chili powder or to taste* 2 mL
> 1 cup *Half and Half* 250 mL
> 1/2 cup *salsa* 125 mL
> 10 oz *Monterey Jack cheese, grated* 375 mL
> 1 *4-oz can mild green chilies, drained and chopped* 125 mL
> *Hot-pepper sauce to taste*
> *Fresh cilantro*

Place butter, flour, onion, and chili powder in a 1-qt (1-L) bowl with pour spout. Microwave, uncovered, at High 2 minutes. Stir. Whisking constantly, gradually pour in Half and Half. Add salsa, cheese, green chilies, and pepper sauce. Microwave at High 2 minutes. Stir. Microwave at Medium-High (70%) 3 to 4 minutes or until cheese melts, stirring once. Garnish with cilantro and serve with shrimps, scallops, and vegetables for dipping. Makes 2 cups (500 mL) dip.

Note: If possible, use a fondue pot or warming tray to keep dip warm.

Crab-Stuffed Mushroom Caps

Use the crab mixture to stuff celery or serve it with crackers or vegetables as a dip.

24 *medium-size mushrooms, stems removed* 24
Crab Stuffing:
2 cups *crab meat* 500 mL
1 *8-oz pkg cream cheese* 250 g
2 tbsp *chili sauce or catsup* 25 mL
2 tbsp *chopped green onion* 25 mL
1/3 cup *mayonnaise* 75 mL
Few drops *Tabasco Sauce* Few drops
Chopped fresh parsley (optional)

Place cream cheese in a bowl. Microwave, uncovered, at Medium (50%) 1 to 2 minutes to soften. Add remaining ingredients; combine well. Fill mushroom caps with mixture and arrange in a circle on a round platter. Leave a space between mushrooms. Make a second row, same as first, but leave center of platter empty. When ready to serve, microwave, uncovered, at High 2 to 3 minutes or until mushrooms are hot. Makes 2 cups (500 mL) stuffing.

Variation: If desired, hold stuffing until serving time, then microwave, uncovered, at Medium (70%) 3 to 4 minutes. Garnish with parsley if desired and serve as a dip with crackers or vegetables.

Tortilla Tangers

Tortilla chips make a great base for hot snacks from the microwave. In our house, we have different tastes, so we like to make up our own creations: salsa, shrimp, and grated Monterey Jack for him; crab, green onion, and grated sharp Cheddar for her. Try the following.

1-1/2 cups *grated Cheddar cheese* 375 mL
1 *4-oz can diced green chili peppers, drained* 125 g
1/4 cup *sliced, pitted ripe olives, drained* 50 mL
1/4 cup *sliced green onion* 50 mL
1/4 cup *mayonnaise or salad dressing* 50 mL
1 *4-oz can baby shrimp, drained and rinsed* 125 g
36 to 40 *round tortilla chips* 36 to 40

In a large bowl, combine cheese, chili peppers, olives, onion, and mayonnaise. Gently fold in shrimp. Arrange half of tortilla chips on a platter. Top each chip with 1 rounded tsp (5 mL) cheese mixture. Microwave, uncovered, at High 1 to 2 minutes or until cheese melts, turning platter halfway through. Prepare and microwave a second batch.

Neptune Potato Skins

Homemade or from the freezer, potato skins are a pop-in-your-mouth favorite with any crowd.

Baked potatoes (see Index)
Melted butter
Soy sauce

Cut baked potatoes into quarters lengthwise and then in half to form eight wedges. Scoop out pulp, leaving 1/8 to 1/4 inch (3 mm) skin intact. Brush both sides with melted butter and soy sauce. Bake in conventional oven at 400°F (200°C) until crisp.

Variations: Place shrimp on each baked skin, top with a dab of salsa and grated Monterey Jack cheese. Lay on a platter and microwave, uncovered, at High until cheese melts.

Or top each skin with sour cream and caviar, smoked oysters, sardines, or caper-stuffed anchovies.

Quick Clam Dip

Use vegetables or crackers to scoop up this delicious dip.

1 *8-oz pkg cream cheese* 250 mL
1 *8-oz can minced clams, drained* 250 mL
3 tbsp *milk or cream* 50 mL
1 tbsp *prepared horseradish* 15 mL
2 tsp *minced onion* 10 mL
1 tsp *lemon juice* 5 mL
1/4 tsp *garlic salt* 1 mL
1/4 tsp *paprika* 1 mL
1/8 tsp *pepper* 0.5 mL
Celery leaves for garnish

Place cream cheese in a 1-1/2-qt (1.5-L) serving dish. Microwave at High, uncovered, 1 to 2 minutes, to soften cheese. Blend in remaining ingredients. Microwave at High 3 to 5 minutes or until heated through, stirring at halfway point. Garnish with celery leaves and serve. Makes 2-1/2 cups (625 mL) dip.

INDEX